Net Net

STORIES FROM A LIFELONG PURSUIT

A memoir by Joan Bigwood

For Muggins

TABLE OF CONTENTS

Foreword

I was eight years old, fidgeting on the sidewalk outside of the house. It's possible my father had just pulled away from the curb on a business trip, or they were inside cleaning up after a dinner party from the night before. I remember the thought I had at that moment better than what brought me into the kitchen just five minutes ago: *I wish I could do two things like my dad. I wish I could sweat like him, and I wish I could tell funny stories like him.*

Sweat

After a morning of gardening, or an afternoon table-tennis match, my father could down most of a glass of lemonade in one go. Cheering madly, I would time how long it took for the lemonade to reappear through the pores in his extended arms. I wished I could do that with my lemonade. Be careful what you wish for.

Funny Stories

They just kept coming. Like the man who was forever leaving his umbrellas on the train. One day he heard the railway was holding an auction for lost umbrellas. He bought an entire lot of umbrellas to replace the ones he had lost over the years. And left the bundle on the train! Or the man who wanted to travel by train from his tiny suburb of Brussels to Peking. Or the chap who offered to do a swallow dive into a bucket. Stories of his time in the Royal Corps of Engineers, literally cleaning up after the British troops who had been stationed in Greece; his company was tasked with removing all the latrines. On his last afternoon in Athens, he sprinted up to the Acropolis because he knew his mother would expect a full report. Those stories starred Muggins, which was another one of his kooky British terms, and means "me." (*Guess who had to clean it all up? Muggins!*) He had a million of 'em.

I have twenty-five. And a couple of those were donated. My stories are by and large true—the names have been changed (family members excepted) for propriety. These stories are held together by a luminescent thread of searing recall. They have formed

2

me, informed me, and in some cases, reformed me. Oh sure, I have plenty of stories that don't involve the handle of a racquet, but the more I thought about the ones I wanted to share with *my public*, the more racquet sports just kept creeping into the picture.

Do you know the old cliché, *this piece of work is a love letter to [insert collective noun]*? Well, this collection really *is* a love letter to racquet sports. That's why I wrote it. Not because I thought anyone else would want to read it, except maybe my 92-year-old aunt who played tennis in college, or my mother's even older childhood bestie who played mixed doubles well into her eighties. I wrote it because when you love the way I love racquet sports, you want to shout it from the rooftops.

Dear racquets, paddles, and every bouncing orb,
Thanks for all the good times. I love you!
(Read on for proof.)

I was a three-sport athlete in high school. My big brother would contend that for a girl in the 1970s, that was not nearly the feat it would be today. I must agree. I was a loud-mouthed soccer goalkeeper who stood around a lot in between heroic leaps, a red-faced and puffing playmaker on the basketball court, and a big-boned first baseman who hit doubles. My mother had zero interest in my sporting career. My father always inquired after my games, feigning interest in these inglorious battles, and chortling indulgently at embarrassing scores (especially in soccer, when I was the deciding factor), ever reminding me not to take any of the outcomes too seriously.

But there was one sport my British father took very seriously, and that was tennis, in all its permutations: table tennis, paddle tennis, badminton (which he did not pronounce *badmitten*, so neither do we), squash, even that-game-you-play-on-the-beach-with-wooden-paddles-and-a-squishy-ball. Dad maintained that if you could play a good game of tennis, you would always get along in life. He really believed this. We are not talking about the kind of getting along that involves golfing with clients all day and sealing deals— we are talking about making friends. Simply that. He used to say, *it would be far harder to organize a softball game than a tennis match.*

Perhaps we humans do come in breeds, and mine involves racquets because in tennis I do not loiter. I will chase down any ball, any time, under almost any circumstances as if it were bred into me. Short shots? Overhead lobs? I win every fair race. For all my "three sports" growing up, the one that would stick the hardest is the one I only ever played on the side. It is also the one that has taught me the most.

Dad and I had an ongoing bet in tennis: $1 to beat him in a game and $5 if I ever took a set off him. I won the game eventually, but it wasn't until I was forty years old that I finally won a set. I called my little brother with the news and his response was

"You beat a 75-year-old man? That wasn't very nice."

(My sister Kate made the racquet and visor.)

Dad, I did as you instructed; I kept up my tennis. Fifty years after I first picked up a racquet, I moved clear across the country to a town in New Hampshire where I knew absolutely no one—yet by the time the holidays rolled around, we were throwing a party for all our new tennis friends.

It's comforting to know there are people you can call to ask for a game, secure they will say yes if they are free. It's the pure height of enjoyment playing a hard match, encouraging each other, and striving to improve together, even from opposite sides of the net.

Tennis, pickleball, squash...even badminton—there's somewhere you can go where, with time and very little effort, everyone will know your name. *Very little effort* is relative—but the effort comes with the sport, not the social stress, so it's a twofer! You improve your game, and guaranteed, you will come out of the experience with a community. Nobody promised you a new best friend at every stage of life, but you *will* have a holiday party to attend. Most likely you will be bringing a White Elephant gift. And taking something equally fabulous home. I have that. And you can, too.

I can still hear Dad's hybrid English accent when I placed a ball just out of his reach: *Shot!* Or when announcing the score at 30-30: *Thirty each apiece all around!* I can feel the early morning mist cool my teenage arms as I practiced my cross-court forehand with a Belgian girl. I can recall the heat on my crimson cheeks when the door to my changing room started to swing open. Net net, I could never have anticipated the trove of stories that my inherited passion for racquet sports would deliver, stretching from South Africa to the Philippines. I hope they inspire others to see racquet sports not only as lifelong pursuits, but as an infinity of valuable life lessons. And lifelong friends! I started a weekly game with a mommy from our kids' elementary school. Twenty years later, I refuse to delete our standing game on my electronic calendar (Thursdays at 8 a.m. Pacific Time) even though we live some 2,000 miles apart, because it reminds me of a lovely stretch of years tending to our inconsistent tennis skills and to our inconsistent offspring in our spare time :)

To my father, may he rest in everlasting power, I will close by saying those three words a parent never tires of hearing: *you were right*. When everything is new, you always have your hobbies, and so do the friends you haven't met yet, with whom you will share them. Now get out there and give it your best grip.

Court *Étique*

When I was ten and my big brother Peter was twelve, he decided it was time to teach me to play tennis. My family was fortunate to belong to one of the most beautiful tennis clubs in America—in the top 50, according to Tennis Magazine back in the 1970s. You had to wear whites to play, though at the end of a good match, most outfits were a pink hue from the clay dust. We belonged to the New Haven Lawn Club not so much for the clay courts as for the fancy restaurant and hotel rooms in the clubhouse, where my father hosted out-of-town clients. He represented European companies, and the New Haven Lawn Club made the right impression when his associates came across the pond to check out his operation. My mother used the club as a babysitting service, since she worked full time at Yale, and summers in New Haven in the 60s and 70s were long and hot. My day started at six in the morning with swim team practice and ended sometime around five, coinciding with when Mom was making her way home from work.

Peter chose one such sweltering summer day to school me in his very favorite sport. What a labor of love this started out to be! If I managed to actually connect with the ball, it would *sproing* off out of bounds, or over the back fence, or into the net, but rarely into his side of the court where my long-suffering brother stood in his baggy shorts and polo shirt, calling out technical advice that I would ignore. Tennis in the first hours is a game of reckless inefficiency. It is best played against a wall, or at least with someone equally pathetic because no one should have to endure those inevitably terrible shots unless they, too, are only capable of the same or worse. To play with a beginner is to care; it is to have hope in a brighter future.

Unlike a toddler taking its first steps, with that mix of intense concentration and utter rapture, I felt nothing but rage and self-loathing as a tennis newbie. For every lame swipe, I tumbled further into pre-adolescent despair. I got hotter, pinker, sloppier and more and more enraged. My discomfort was only intensified by the pulsating purity of my opponent, who stood lightly in place, watching me chase down errant shots. The damper my hand-me-down tennis shirt, the dustier my ankles, the more pristine his bright white form.

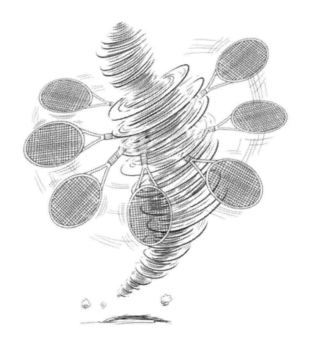

The more erratic my game, the more centered and calm my brother appeared. When my lesson mercifully ended, we rode home in silence, me pedaling furiously to keep up with his high gears. I went straight to my room to sulk, as was my custom, and which inevitably ended with me snoring lightly. Later, when Mom was home from work and we were irritating her in the kitchen before dinner, Peter sighed heavily. I could tell the sigh was directed at me. I winced and checked the exits, as one practiced in avoiding trouble.

"Joanie doesn't have court *étique*," young Peter declared. There was a pause. I was lost, but that was normal. What wasn't normal was to see our mother looking confused. Then enlightenment.

"I think you mean etiquette, dear."

Having no idea what court *eteek*, nor indeed *etikett* meant, I went with an old standard:

"HA HA you said *eteek!* Court *eteek* hahaha!" And danced out of the kitchen before anyone could instruct me in proper etiquette. Fifty years later, I have learned nearly everything there is to know about court etiquette, but court *étique,* is far more nuanced. Court *étique* is everything *else* racquet sports have taught me over the years and miles. *Étique* is the octogenarian of my youth, a surrogate grandfather, who would jog slower than I walk around his dining-room table until he achieved a mile, to keep fit for his weekly tennis lesson. It is the stranger at the Caribbean resort who is looking for a game and finds you, looking too. It is the friendly handshake at the end of a gruesome match. Court *étique* is the longing to win when you know you are being creamed. And the slight embarrassment of beating someone who is better than you but is not playing their best. Or the discomfort of walloping someone who is not up to your level.

Through racquet sports I have encountered diligence, kindness, passion, heartache, fetishism, obsession, depression, dementia, deference, integrity, community, but most especially, love.

I want to share that love with you.

The Ladies' Locker Room .

The New Haven Lawn Club may have been a status symbol for those families who dropped in from time to time on their way in and out of town from their second homes and expensive summer camps, but for those of us who spent every waking hour of our summers there, it was more of a colony, where we may have been subject to foreign rule (our parents *in absentia*) but were otherwise free to establish our own society. The "we" in question were all under the age of 16.

Most of us were pre-teens. We went from swim team practice to the playground, where we could still tuck our feet up just enough to enjoy mad swinging sessions, where the chains that held our canvas seats clanged with the heights we attained. When we got bored, we trudged off to the Wall with our racquets and scavenged old tennis balls for some erratic practice. Then back to the pool, over to the snack bar, maybe to a back court for a game of doubles, then back to the pool after a sweaty, grimy match. During the sporadic downpours of a New England summer, we would sneak into the ballroom for some fine theatrics, or down to the squash courts for a little alone time. If it was a quiet day at the club, we might retreat to the elegantly appointed, very formal Ladies' Locker Room up in the main clubhouse.

It wasn't all gentility and grace at the club. One of the first times I dared breach the inner sanctum of the Ladies' Locker Room, I was with kids I didn't know all that well, kids from other parts of town. When the heavens opened that afternoon, scattering tennis players and families who had come for a swim, one of these girls got the bright idea that we lay siege on the Ladies' Locker Room for some good old-fashioned fun, before pre-scheduled rides would be showing up from the suburbs.

We snuck up through the empty halls of the wedding and banqueting facilities and fairly pranced into the Ladies' Locker Room undetected. With all the rain, it was blessedly empty that afternoon. It smelled of women's beauty and warm, clean hair. Nothing like the stale-water stench of the overcrowded dressing rooms down in the pool area. We knew we weren't supposed to play in there. The fainting couches and vanities were reserved for the very serious business of being ladies. But we felt somehow exceptional, because of the rain.

We changed out of our whites since the courts wouldn't be dry again until the next day. Since we didn't really know each other, we put on our bathing suits for group showers, followed by foot races around the lockers, a chaotic roller derby in club-issued paper slippers. It was heady stuff, turning one way or another, and having a new friend in every direction.

As I slid around the corner of a bank of lockers, my giddiness downshifted into agony at the sight of one of my new friends waving my underpants, then flinging them into the air in one triumphant motion, to land on top of the lockers. Another grabbed my tennis shorts, cackling, and tossed them up to join the underpants.

Was this bullying? Had I been caught in an elaborate snare? Their giggles were breathless and menacing. I smiled stiffly, out of breath and confused, and snatched up my shirt before it was launched. Then the girls ran off—it was that quick—leaving behind a shell of my former self in my team swimsuit and paper slippers, shuffling over to my socks and sneakers, a pounding pulse in an ill-fitting dressing room. Yet somehow comforting. I sat in that powdery world as if in the bosom of a grandma. Then I fashioned a towel skirt to wear through the club's formal reception area, and out the main door before anyone could apprehend me for the dress code violation. Down the driveway I trudged, then veered into the lower parking lot and to the entrance to the pool area, where the rain had closed down the carnival atmosphere. My new 'friends' were very much gone. I borrowed the phone at the desk and called my mother at work. I was comforted by the alarm in her voice when I announced that I had just been bullied. This was a new experience for her, too.

I waited in a spare chair at the front desk, out of the drizzle. I sat and picked my cuticles while table umbrellas were stowed and the snack bar was locked up. Mom showed up on her way home from work and walked me up to the Ladies' Locker Room. Not being a tennis player, nor even much of a swimmer, my mother had probably never even darkened the door. Yet she located a wire hanger and unwound it enough to fish my clothes off the lockers. There was a grimness to her that made me feel oddly at fault. I felt like a girl in a book, whose own mother hardly knew her anymore. She recommended I find new friends. I nodded, realizing I didn't even know these girls' last names. But I also realized that just because you know someone, doesn't mean they're your friend. And you will get to decide what it means to be a friend over and over your whole life long. Maybe it was only meant to be a harmless prank. I had just undergone an initiation that I felt sure I had passed, not because I didn't cry in their presence but because I timed my rescue for after they had all gone home. We didn't end up crossing paths much after that. Travel and camps and then late-summer, off to our respective schools. Some experiences just wake you up to truths about the human race you never knew. That keeps happening, by the way. It's OK, though. Keep going.

Number Two Doubles

I wore my tomboyishness like a badge. In a twisted interpretation of *If you can't beat 'em, join 'em*, I met my brother Peter's aloof superiority with a fearless determination to prove myself worthy of his company. If he set out to build a go-kart, I would volunteer as his engine. I learned to not "throw like a girl" so he would let me play *Steal the Base* with him and his friends. I was usually the runner, and took a few scorchers to the ol' noggin, but that only upped my approval ratings. I swaggered like Peter, I hitched up my jeans like him, I even wiped my nose on my sleeve. At age nine, I convinced a group of boys in our new neighborhood that I was a boy by climbing up to the roof of our house (I climbed out of an attic window and sashayed around to the front where they could make out my triumphant pose). They finally believed me.

Nothing about femininity appealed, except kissing boys, that is. I was as boy crazy as the next set of XX chromosomes, but my approach was wildly different. While other girls were investing in hair product and skin tonics, short skirts and glossy, plump braids, I learned how to throw a football, ice skate with hockey skates, and make a lay-up on a give-and-go play. I honed my sassy wisecracks. I took a joke. To be rigorously honest here, I felt more like a closeted gay boy in middle school. In after-school games of touch football, mangy boys in worn corduroys drew plays on my chest with their stubby fingers as I gulped for air, fighting off a swoon. These boys may have been taken with sweet-smelling girls in knee socks and kilts, but they were largely inconvenienced by these girls' attentions. Attention, not so much. Attentions, not so fast. Boys in middle school were devoted to their burgeoning, wide-ranging interests, which mostly involved blowing off steam. I was there for their steam. It ran the go-kart engine that was me.

Photographer: Unknown Yalie

One 'friendboy' had me over to his home after a game of tennis. He lived in one of the Yale colleges (grand gothic halls of residence surrounding central squares dotted around New Haven) where his father was the Head of College. We were hanging around the quad in our tennis whites playing some boyish game that involved dirt, rocks, and explosion noises, when an undergrad approached us, asking if he could take our photo. It seems that we were remarkably filthy, except for my bright white tennis hat.

"You boys wait here. I'll go get my camera." We used the time to smear even more dirt on ourselves. When the earnest young photographer returned, I had to lean forward with my elbows on my knees for the portrait, because at this point, my chest was beginning to sprout. It was a given that we would not be letting him in on the secret. Soon my mother would be buying me training bras and my life would become one huge existential conundrum. I did ultimately transition, if not in the traditional sense, from a tomboy to a card-carrying woman; it took birthing my first child for the process to be complete. Truly. It took thirty years. Nursing played a major role.

When I was 17, post-puberty but still loping around in a jean jacket deemphasizing any curves, I joined a couple of 18-year-old friends at a bar in New Haven by flashing my brother's driver's license (they didn't come with photos back then) at the bouncer. Once inside, the bartender also demanded to see my license, accusing me of "not even shaving yet." I had tricked him into accepting me as Peter, just not as of legal age.

That same summer, I played on our club tennis team in the Number Two Doubles slot. My partner was everything a girl on a tennis court should be. Fine-featured, bronzed, sporting shoulder-length chestnut hair which she wore in a fetching high ponytail, her form-fitting tennis dresses grazed her upper thighs like a valance accenting a view of sloping hills. When she hit a forehand, her free hand measured the distance from the ground to her hip like a ball-jointed doll with dainty painted nails. Did I mention she was very pretty? No one would argue the point, no matter what their conception of beauty. You simply couldn't fault her. To top it all off, she had a big handsome boyfriend who came to watch our matches. I wanted a big handsome boyfriend to watch me play tennis. Not that I would have known what to do with one after the match, other than arm-wrestle or fall asleep watching Saturday Night Live.

I was undeniably cowed by my partner's pristine perfection. By now I knew the term 'androgynous,' and identified perfectly with its definition of an indeterminate gender—not the harder-core hermaphrodite—but certainly a woman-child of other attributes than traditional girlishness. I knew I wasn't whatever this pretty, pretty princess was, floating around the court like a dessert topping. I was tougher, messier, sweatier. I was still sharing my big brother's polo shirts and whatever white shorts I could grab from the dryer. I felt like the sideshow to her main attraction. But here's the best part. We were a powerhouse twosome. Our strategy on the court was remarkably complementary. She delivered on smooth baseline strokes, and I came out of nowhere at the net with the punchy finish. We won all our matches that summer. It turns out it takes all types to make up a winning combination. This compensated for the fact that we had to share her boyfriend as our number-one fan.

Two years later, home from college for Winter Break, I attended a local New Year's Eve party in dressy white satin trousers and an electric blue blouse. Who should be there but my former tennis partner's now former boyfriend. We talked all evening, trading snarky observations and collaborating on punchlines. At the end of the night, he stood before me, eyes sparkling. He informed me that he would be heading back to college the next day, but he wanted me to know that he had *never met a girl like me*. This came as no surprise, but this time, I saw myself not so much as "other," but as uniquely me. I had come full circle with that big handsome boyfriend of the summer of Number Two Doubles, when I had felt deeply like Number Two. That late December night, I felt like Number One Singles.

Chez Courtois

One could argue this story started when my father was rushed out of bed and into a taxi headed to *Bruxelles-Midi* to board a train to Lisbon on May 10, 1940—my grandfather's company had a shadow office set up in Portugal on account of the fascist menace—but their escape was interrupted later that day by a fire on the railroad tracks as France, too, fell to the Germans. My father's train uncoupled from the luggage car and traveled backwards to Boulogne, where my grandparents managed to secure passage for their family of five on a destroyer to England with nothing but that day's clothes. It was off to their country of origin, where incidentally they had scarcely lived over several generations, now refugees in their motherland, in Weston-Super-Mare. Or Weston-Super-Nightmare, as my father called it.

If my story begins there, it picks up when my father and his older brother returned to Brussels after the war, leaving their much younger sister and parents behind in England in favor of their childhood idyll, the Brussels of picnics in the *Bois de la Cambre*, bicycles that jounced over cobblestones, and friendly pick-up football matches in empty streets with wholesome boys named Henri or Arnaud. Now trained engineers, the brothers would seek their fortune where they had once been so comfortable and unconcerned. They were now men rebuilding a battle-worn city. But Dear Old Dad had to go and fall in love with a saucy Yank who worked as a "cookie pusher" for the American Foreign Service, a secretary with a mean typing speed, and before he could say *but I just got home* they were sailing to the U.S. for bigger and better opportunities. Babies followed. Dad worked in international business and brought my mother's maternity clothes to his baby sister in England, as she was in the family way. The telegram he received upon his arrival—BRING BACK MATERNITY CLOTHES—set the tone for my childhood. I was the pleasant afterthought. When you are a happy surprise, you tend to live up to your reputation and I was built for the part. My father's nickname for me was Sunshine. The idea was I could eclipse the vilest of weathers with my big, happy smile. In that mode of pleasing an easily pleased father, I was packed off for the summer to Brussels at the age of 13, to stay with a family—an associate of my uncle—to immerse myself in French, the only mother tongue that mattered to my displaced dad. I didn't have much choice in those days, so much as attitude. It was determined that I had a good attitude, and a strong aptitude for French. So it was that my mother tucked me into a hired car in New Haven, Connecticut pointed to JFK for a flight to Belgium via Montreal (and no doubt Reykjavik for re-fueling), whence I was expected to come back fluent in my father's mother tongue.

I can still see her frantically waving from the curb, as my warm tears raced down burning cheeks to a quivering chin. Seeing Sunshine drenched in precipitation, she couldn't contain the news that there was a surprise waiting for me. How I passed the two hours taking me further from home I don't know, though part of it was spent staring out the window wondering what I could have possibly done to deserve this exile. Privilege is wasted on the young, I know that now, but at the time, the smelly, low-slung, beat-up old limousine packed with strangers heading to New York felt more like a paddy wagon. I had forgotten all about the surprise when I got to my terminal. I shifted from my seat, slippery with sweat, was handed a much-too large suitcase, and turned bravely to make my way inside, when I heard the distinct British-Belgian bass tones of my father: *is this the young lady traveling to Europe?*

He had detoured to the airport on his way back from a business trip. Perhaps the story begins at the ticket counter, where the agent dully informed us that my flight was delayed, that I was in jeopardy of missing my connection in Montreal. When she denied any responsibility on the part of the airline for my well-being should I be stranded in Canada overnight, my father's hand slammed so hard on her countertop that she immediately turned to get help. He walked away in a maroon rage, dragging me behind. I had thought that brand of spittle-spraying fury was reserved only for domestic discipline when we acted with anything short of the unquestioning obedience of the pre-war European children of Dad's upbringing. It turned out airline employees could also bring about that startling smack of hand meat on the nearest surface, principally bare bottoms. I could sense his bestial protectiveness. All I wanted was to resurrect my sweet-natured father and make him happy, once again.

But for me this story begins at the dinner table of Monsieur and Madame Courtois and their three pallid offspring, Véronique, Yves and Christiane, after a very long journey with a much-too-heavy suitcase, now sharing my first meal of the summer of 1974 with a table of strangers, a bewildered refugee.

We had spent a year in Brussels when I was five, trying to repatriate our father of four whose innocence was wrested from him on May 10, 1940. A year of strange customs and flavors, of marzipan and men pissing on walls did little to prepare me for the tomato served to me on my first night nine years later, gutted and crammed with grey crustaceans that smelled like a dirty fish tank and which I would come to find out was a Belgian delicacy: *Tomate aux Crevettes*. This was not a dish I was willing, nay, able to stomach and was consequently forced to declare myself "*allergique.*" It was obvious no one believed me, however plausible it seemed at the time. Munching on bread and cheese, I made up for my gastronomic reticence with conversational derring-do, turning to Monsieur Courtois, and asking him if he traveled with his work.

Had this been my household, and a newly minted teenager from a foreign land had ventured to launch a conversation in my native language, I would have forgiven the allergy gambit and rewarded her with a slow, careful response, choosing vocabulary words I would assume she had picked up in her language lessons: *yes, I travel sometimes outside of the city and sometimes outside of the country*. Extraordinarily, my first conversational bid *chez Famille* Courtois was met with an outburst of laughter, yes laughter, not *with*, but *at* me. I had addressed Monsieur Courtois in the familiar form, what is reserved for friends and people of lower status. I had called him *tu* rather than *vous* and the family explained between gasps that *tu* never went with *Monsieur*. It is impossible to convey the sinking feeling that washed over the whole of me as I faced down some 100 days with these jackals, who served me delicacies that looked like the cat regurgitated them into a hollowed-out tomato, while laughing at my efforts to communicate with them in their fast-paced tongue.

The sun in Sunshine set that night. If they were going to laugh at my attempts at connection, I would simply unplug altogether, retreating into the panic room of my psyche. When I should have been babysitting neighbors' kids poolside, and holding hands in movie theaters, I was consigned to the misery of a Belgian household where the parents would fight loudly, the kids incessantly, and my mastery of the local lingo was, literally, at a grade-school level.

Word had spread around my hometown that I needed mail—my mother wrote me several times a week, chronicling her uneventful life to fill the page and drop in the mailbox. School friends would find time to send me reports of boring days missing me. I was grateful for their kindness, and for their boredom. Back in 1974, letters overseas came in folded self-sealing blue paper

packets called Aerogrammes. I lived for these sweet offerings. The eldest Courtois, Véronique, a non-communicative (unless she was screaming at her siblings) 16-year-old, saw me sitting on a retaining wall behind the house, re-reading one of my blue letters and asked me in a hiss if I memorized them. The 14-year-old son, closest in age to me, was what we call in French a *pleurnichard,* or cry-baby. Board games inevitably ended with him storming off crying. To this day I can say 1) "It's not your turn," 2) "You're a cheater," 3) "I quit!" and 4) "Shut your face!" with an agility that would fool any Francophone. In fact, when I got back from that summer and started high school, I was placed in a third-year honors French class due to all my progress in Belgium. I did have to be gently reprimanded when I responded to the teacher's invitation to choose which part to read in a theatrical scene with what loosely translates as:

"I don't give a f*ck, Madame."

One night after dinner *chez* Courtois, we had all eaten our containers of yogurt, and I think I was the one who replaced the foil top on mine and returned it to the center of the table, such that it looked perfectly untouched. (I was not a prankster by nature but was seized by so many unfamiliar impulses that summer I hardly knew what I was by the start of high school. Though come to think of it, does anyone?) When Yves the *pleurnichard* noticed what appeared to be an unopened yogurt, he reached for it, only to discover as he snatched it up that it was empty. Again, he was reduced to self-pitying sobs as the family laughed uproariously.

Christiane, twelve, and generally unlikeable, was assigned to me. I even had to share a bath with this boney child when we went to their stone farmhouse outside of Brussels on the weekends. I remember once again sitting on a retaining wall, this time watching microscopic red insects beetle around the stone, thinking why would anyone come here for their enjoyment? The mere notion of a 'weekend house' fills me with an inexplicable dread that until this moment I had never connected to that crumbling stone pile. There was quite literally nothing to do there. The rooms were scarcely furnished, bathwater was at a premium, and I cannot remember one single thing we did from Saturday to Sunday afternoon. For all intents and purposes Monsieur and Madame Courtois simply needed a change of scene for their constant bickering.

Christiane never addressed me with her eyes open. Instead, as she swiveled her head in my general direction, her eyelids would raise like a curtain on a repertoire of blank expressions. She had several, like the much older Véronique, who also shared with her baby sister aggressive armpit hair that sprouted early in the season, shall we say. No woman in the household seemed to own a razor. Christiane's prattle could have held me back that summer, for I tended to ignore her, but in fact she made me excel. Not because of superior pedagogy, don't get me wrong. If ever I made a mistake, Christiane would stop everything, like a symphony conductor on a false note and would use the teaching moment as a platform for her vast linguistic superiority, this *twelve-year old* in her *native tongue.* I was about to turn *fourteen.* Consequently, I tried very hard to never make an error in her presence. That extended to the household; if I didn't know where the salt and pepper shakers were stored, *par exemple,* I would ask Yves. Christiane may have been ahead of me in French (and armpit hair), but I was still older and that simply had to count for something. (Sadly, it did make me Yves' peer, which I found *dégueulasse,* or vomitose.)

One day, coming up the stairs from the cellar with two bottles of water for Madame Courtois, I espied in the corner of the landing two dusty old wooden tennis racquets in their presses. It was the equivalent of Harry Potter finding an unassuming but highly potent talisman. Like the wily Harry, I was careful not to show too much interest in the racquets, for fear they would be denied me. I didn't trust any situation that summer. The racquets had belonged to the grandparents, who were in a home now. (The direct translation is actually "a house." They lived in "a house for the olds.") I would use the racquets to put Christiane in her place once and for all.

Monsieur Courtois carefully explained that the racquets were worth nothing. He had intended to consign them to the garbage can. It took me a few hours to gather up the nerve to ask if we could borrow the racquets all the same. Addressing him with the formality that expressed my lowly status in his oppressive family structure, I persuaded him that we would only be playing like babies (an actual expression, at least in their home), and that the terrible racquets owned by the olds would serve us sufficiently. It worked. Monsieur Courtois decided to allow me to learn my lesson by temporarily relinquishing his right to throw them out. He rolled his eyes just the way his eldest daughter did as he painfully bent over the dusty old racquets. He even had a can of tennis balls tucked away. Later that afternoon, I got Yves to show me where to find cleaning rags. I wanted to dust off and check for warping for this, the first thing that felt like an adventure that summer.

It took some convincing before Yves allowed us to borrow his unloved bicycle to ride to the cracked tennis court in a nearby park. Like his father, he could not bring himself to support this outrageous misuse of trashed tennis racquets. If the self-effacing house guest hadn't humbled herself to near abasement to get that bike, we would still be waiting for his permission.

I was only thirteen when I first experienced something that I would come to know as my secret power (not to be confused with a superpower). A secret power is that delicious inner knowing that you have, in spite of the sense that you are drowning in defeat, *one* tiny but significant fact about yourself, which carries you through. In this foreign land among psychic vampires intent on draining my lifeblood, I could still hold my racquet with the right grip for a deep topspin. I could fairly feel my imaginary cape undulating in the wind as we biked to the park. I would show Christiane not only my superior skill, but I would show her how to teach a beginner with humility and grace. OK maybe a few weeks later I literally fell on the ground laughing as Christiane whiffed a backhand and went spinning like a top into the fence. But just as in grammar, there are often exceptions to rules.

That summer was nothing if not one gigantic grammar lesson: Subject = I. Object = my summer in Brussels. Transitive verb = to survive. Even riding a bike on someone else's streets put me in touch with my shadow self; the talkative teen with a kind streak, who could crack a joke at twice the speed these people spoke their lazy, short-cut French. With power enough to share graciously, yet living, as she did that summer, in the shadows, she crouched impatiently for some kind of homecoming. On the bike I could pump into the knowledge that I was still in there somewhere, though "I" was a pre-verbal toddler when in the company of the Belgian peoples.

Even Billie Jean King needs to practice, to keep up her skills. I hadn't played an entire school year (except a few games of squash, but that is another story). My mechanics were rusted shut and Christiane could barely coordinate her hand with her eye in opening the gate to the court. Attempting to complete even one two-way exchange with the tennis ball was out of the question. Instead, we stood shoulder to shoulder, shaking hands with our racquets. We practiced the backward C for forehand and a similar backhand with an exaggerated front step. Later, much later in the lesson, I introduced the ball. Even though I was lousy at the spanking-new double-handed backhand of my friends' fancy tennis camps back home, I was seized with the notion that I could teach it to someone else if I explained it carefully.

Something else I learned that summer that had nothing to do with French: with enthusiasm, one can teach what one can't even do oneself.

Sometimes you ease into new habits and other times, you are swept up in a quasi-religious conversion. In the house, we went about our isolationist business, reading, sitting, writing letters home (me) but on the court, Christiane and I were one—a joyful chorus of two practicing a challenging duet. The fresh air, the sun, the mist, the morning dew, the very outsideness of our obsession made it therapeutic. A healthy distance from household tension and from sullen siblings, Christiane was a kite in the wind. The bitter, unresolvable argument that was her parents' marriage was out of earshot. Together, alone on that uneven asphalt we worked on bettering ourselves, snapping wrists on our run-away serves, chasing lobs like commuters catching the last train home. I had absorbed a lot of tennis basics from my big brother by then, and teaching is a great teacher. By the end of the summer, Christiane and I played a set, and she actually won a few points.

Tennis in Brussels is what I remember most fondly about that summer, or at least tennis in Brussels comes in as a close second to scout and guide camp (pronounced *scoot ay gheed)*: DIY camp for two weeks in a French farmer's fields with an enormous group of kids and no one over the age of twenty-one to supervise. It ranks as one of my most memorable lifetime experiences where no racquet was involved; only shovels, used to dig the enormous ditch that paid the farmer for the use of his land.

But back in Brussels, repeating our homemade drills with military precision and crowing at our successes felt so much like home. There was enough shared joy on the court in one hour to surpass a week back at the multi-story emotional maze that was *chez* Courtois. Tennis with Christiane turned out to be our shared secret power.

Kentucky Fried Tennis

When my parents were young marrieds and my eldest brother Jimbo was one, they rented a cottage at the edge of a pond on a large estate in Weston, Connecticut, a forested enclave an hour and change north of New York City. My parents had a knack for sweet deals when they were newly married and poor; with some ingenuity, they landed on their feet time after time. For example, Mom entered a jingle contest for some long-forgotten beauty brand and filled it with product placements and plays on words that won her first prize: two tickets to My Fair Lady on Broadway, starring Rex Harrison and Julie Andrews. There was a two-year waitlist for that show, besides which they could never have afforded such a luxury. *We dined out on that for years!* my father would hoot every time it came up, dining out on it yet again.

For years and years after they moved out of the guesthouse, we went back to Weston on the 4th of July for tennis, swimming, and Kentucky Fried Chicken. The older couple who hosted us were our adopted Auntie Claire and Uncle Paul; the kindest, most gracious WASPs you could meet. Claire was petite, leathery brown and she croaked like a frog from years of social smoking. She

43

even looked a smidge ranine (of or pertaining to frogs, for those of you groping for a dictionary). Her eyes bulged slightly, and her mouth spread wide when she spoke. In the right outfit, she would not have looked out of place pushing an overloaded grocery cart down a grimy sidewalk. But with wealth comes implied glamor and in the context of eye-popping floral upholstery and matching bespoke drapes you would only see a pampered woman of indisputable social standing. Serving the chicken pieces with silver tongs, she made KFC look like *haute cuisine.* Uncle Paul had impeccable posture and a grin that never left his face, standing at the end of the line for chicken parts, ushering everyone in before him, even my equally deferential dad. Auntie Claire and Uncle Paul were the epitome of "comfortable." They had a circular driveway, a sunken living room, a fenced-in tennis court and a stone walkway past the pond and through a patch of woods that led to their out-of-the-way swimming pool, where we four kids would horse around for hours. We could fight, make up, and start a new fight before anyone even remembered to check on us. Sometimes the adult sons of our counterfeit aunt and uncle would come over with their wives and young kids. We'd be on our best behavior around those pampered heirs, making sure nobody drowned in the pool while the adults played non-stop tennis.

Mom didn't play. She "watched," with a good book. But with all the adult offspring and spouses there were plenty to make up doubles teams. We kids would come around in between activities and cheer on our dad, and when my brother Peter was old enough, he got to play, too. It was in Weston when I was first exposed, up-close-and-personal, to the gentility of mixed doubles. These people took court etiquette to a high art, where nearly every closing shot was followed by a good-natured comment, a clever quip, a wink, a gracious aside, or a bolstering word of support. I never heard a single cross word on that court. It was museum-quality sportsmanship. The effect was what milling around a host of angels must be like: just a surfeit of goodwill to all.

Everyone would work up quite an appetite for those buckets of chicken, washed down with thick glass bottles of coke that came in a weathered wooden crate. But first, there were drinks on the brick patio overlooking the pond at the bottom of the sloping back lawn. The afternoon light bronzed the women to perfection in their early July tans. Even Mom looked like a woman of leisure in that light. The men jiggled the ice in their squat drinks as they chuckled and honked their way into the dinner hour. Standing or sitting, they formed the brass section; while the women and children trilled over the day's happenings as the cicadas kept a steady beat. Of all the late afternoons on those bricks, there was for me one stand-out moment. When I was a middle schooler, my mother pulled me close and pointed to one of the comely daughters-in-law.

"Watch how Liza listens. She is an excellent listener."

The coiffed 30-something in a Marimekko shift leaned into her father-in-law's long shadow as he recounted another cheery story from his charmed past. What was especially ironic about this object lesson is my mother was a pretty terrible listener. Decades later, at a table of old ladies at a church supper, she treated everyone to updates on her five grandchildren, whom none of them knew, until I interrupted her by asking the other diners whether *they* had grandchildren. Surprise, surprise, they all did! Maybe my mother knew deep down she couldn't pass on that aural skill and chose perfectly poised Liza to teach me how to listen. Whatever the reason, when I am listening to a gasbag *d'un certain age* going on a little long, I think of that rapt daughter-in-law in the glow of that long-ago brick patio.

Maybe you learn how to behave in polite society on the tennis court. Maybe teaming up with three other cheery souls who play their best but know how to laugh at their mistakes, while maintaining a lighthearted enmity for the opposition, encourage their partners, then trade them at the end of a set like game young swingers...maybe a tennis court is the perfect proving ground for social graces. Mom never picked up a racquet, which might explain her erratic performance off-court. But boy, could she rhyme.

Lingua Franca

I spent my early years trailing after my clever older brother: Peter of the elegant tennis stroke, the syncopated drumming skill, and the flawless delivery of German, which he picked up in high school along with his equally impressive guitar-playing and perfected in college.

I knew a hero when I saw one and for a very long time, Peter was that hero. Not that he ever fell from grace, but at a certain point I had to peel my identity off of his, and make my own way, pursuing my own interests and accomplishments. But well into my 20s, I was still starstruck by the young man who came two years before me in a collection of four larger-than-life children. He was my guiding star throughout my childhood. My sister, two years older than Peter, took after our mother in the sports arena, but excelled at all things indoors. I never felt I shared her skill set but we share other things, like a belly laugh, on a regular basis. Same goes for my eldest brother, whose sport is producing movies. They are all stars in my firmament but only one of them knows what I mean by a split step and slice.

It would not be a stretch to say that I wanted to *be* Peter. If I had been born fifty years later, I suppose I would have been labeled 'gender fluid' and might have been tempted by he/him/his pronouns. I was the Shiloh Jolie-Pitt of my generation minus the designer threads and gorgeous parents.* I was such a tomboy, with my pixie haircuts and droopy jeans, that when I shuffled into a public restroom, women would gasp, to the point where it became routine for me to announce I was a girl before heading to a stall. So boyish that once when I was visiting my best friend's beach house and I needed to borrow a change of shirt, I was horrified to be handed a peasant blouse. Slipping it over my head felt akin to cross-dressing. Not too long ago I saw a photo of that day and was surprised to see two cute little girls in delicate south-of-the-border handwork staring back at me. What does any of this have to do with racquet sports, you may be asking yourself.

If I couldn't *be* Peter, at least I could sound like him. And so, I set off to learn German; *Hoch Deutsch*—High German—the language of Goethe (as opposed to the guttural dialect of his base-born fellow countrymen). I spent the summer at the *Goethe Institut* in a village near Köln.

Late breaking news: Shiloh Jolie-Pitt has been donning dresses! She beat me to it by a football field.

I brought a handful of vocabulary words—the ones I had picked up on Hogan's Heroes, and the one I practically invented when we had a German youth spending the summer at our home (in exchange for my brother's summer at his house in Freiburg). I was pretending to speak cartoon German when he suddenly stopped me.

"You said a real word! *Kugellager*!" It seems that in the middle of all the gibberish I had clearly said "ball bearing."

But back to the *Goethe Institut*, where I arrived by train, clutching a phrase book that spelled out phonetically the necessaries: "excuse me" was *entshooldeegoong*, for example. It looked more like Urdu, and thoroughly confused my right brain as I struggled for weeks to commit the proper spelling, *entschuldigung*, to memory.

In Herr P.'s beginner German class, we were a diverse group of imbeciles. The matching nuns from Spain, the puffy office administrator from Finland who never seemed fully awake, the cocky teenager from a lesser branch of the Saudi royal family, the jaded sprite from Italy with her broken-glass English, the wisecracking college student from Turkey, balding businessmen from Poland, Japan, and Argentina...we were an exotic amalgam. It was a full-immersion program, meaning even on Ground Level I, as ours was called, nothing but German was spoken in the classroom. On the first day, the teacher walked in and addressed the class with the traditional *Guten Morgen*. So far, so good. He then wrote on the board: *Mein Name ist Pflüger*. He picked up a rectangular piece of cardstock from his desk, folded it lengthwise, and with a great show of concentration, wrote Pflüger on either side, creating a table tent nametag. In a show of universal understanding, we all reached for our card stock in front us and wrote our names twice. I remember thinking what a weird name his parents picked for him, as I wrote JOANIE in all caps. It was only after we had all propped up our handmade table tents that I realized *Name* means last name. For the rest of the summer, it was Herr Takahashi, Fräulein Järvinen, Herr Yildiz, Herr Gonzalez, Herr Wiśniewski and Fräulein Joanie. Me and the nuns (Schwester Flora *und* Schwester Maria). Informality coursed through my red, white, and blue veins; viewed by most of the rest of the world as a national religion.

As our language skills strengthened, we gave short presentations. The young Saudi taught us how to train dogs to be killers, by raising them in the dark, and feeding them raw meat. The saucy Turk made himself cry, describing his mother as a true saint, as Schwestern Flora *und* Maria shifted uncomfortably in their seats. Herr Takahashi was incomprehensible. Whenever he spoke, everyone beamed. What else could we do? Communication is a two-way street, and we made a very safe neighborhood. I remember the morning *Fräulein* J. showed up drunk to class. We never let on that she was passed out by *Pause* (break). She roused in time for *Mittagessen* (mid-day-eat).

With scant common language other than mostly poor English, we often chose to spend our time away from the language lab at the table tennis table in the courtyard.

In contrast to the painstaking mastery of *Hoch Deutsch*, there is very little skill required for a friendly game of table tennis. Even the nuns in their trim habits could have a go. Everyone could count to twenty-one in German, no matter their level, scoring in increments of five; so simple, so fool-proof. This was our *lingua franca*. In a shared state of hypnotic mindfulness, we pinged and ponged the afternoon away, at last free of the exhausting internalization of cases, tenses and correct pronunciation. Here, drunkenness in class was no more than a forgotten dream. The lesser Saudi royal with the killer dogs was but a clumsy southpaw with an inferiority complex, and the teary Turk was his old smart-ass self. International businessmen who needed German for their very livelihood, to run subsidiaries and raise families far from their homelands, went up against a dilettante who simply, fiercely, wanted to sound like her/his brother. Table tennis, the great equalizer, brought together the nations of the world and gave us each a hallowed place, against a lulling metronome of bat to ball to table, to bat again.

At the end of a long summer of increasing linguistic independence, we were put together with all the other levels of students in a room for a "mocktail party" as a way of putting into *praxis* our sturdy phrases. One surefire conversation starter, *Was sind Sie von Beruf?* (What do you do for work?) led, much to my inordinate delight to an exchange with a man from Level III, who answered:

"*Wir machen Kugellager,*" to which I nodded sagely. His company made ball bearings.

Nachtischtennis

I turned twenty-one in a tiny West German town near Mannheim, where I spent the summer working in the export department of a local steel firm, one of my father's long-time clients. I was there to improve my German, but like an embedded spy, I left with so much more than language proficiency. It is impossible to quantify all that happened to me that summer, that to this day is still happening...but it all started at a ping pong table.

NB: I was raised to call the sport not the traditional ping pong, but "table tennis," and this is, in fact, its name in German: *Tischtennis*. (Clever non-German-speaking reader, you now know three words in German: *Tisch* is table, *Tennis* is self-explanatory and now *Tischtennis*.) For the sake of my late British father's unwavering insistence, I will only refer to it by its proper name, the name of my childhood: table tennis.

Table tennis is a big part of my personal history, especially that summer in Ketsch: population some 12,000, nestled in an oxbow of the Rhine River in the region of Rhein-Neckar-Kreis in Baden-Württemberg, the Southwest corner of pre-1989 West Germany.

When I first arrived at the narrow stucco house with the flowerboxes that spilled technicolor geraniums onto an otherwise blank, deserted main street, I had a sit-down with the *Hausfrau,* the beloved Frau G., as to what we eat for breakfast in America. Yes, we eat cornflakes, yes, we eat ham and eggs, yes, we eat toast and jam, yes, we drink coffee, though I prefer tea...but anything at all would be fine. From that day forward she served me all of those things for breakfast, every day. Fortunately for me I went running after work because I would not have fit into any of my clothes by summer's end (clothes that she laundered and ironed for me while I was at work, including my underwear).

The second thing that dominates my recollection of that first day and every day thereafter was the table tennis after dinner. It took place nightly after *Schnapps,* which I refused, for the first month, anyway. The only time up to that point that I had tasted *Schnapps* was when our father brought back a bottle of Pear Williams from a trip to West Germany, a frosted bottle with a luscious pear pictured on the label. It had a divine pear smell, but to my virgin tongue, tasted like the firewater of lore. In fact, I tricked my big brother into taking a proper swallow by wetting my upper lip and gulping loudly, rhapsodizing about the yummy pear flavor. I can't remember if he threw it back up, though I suspect he did. But back to Ketsch: it should be noted that by the end of a tough summer, failing rather miserably at office work in a difficult language, I was accepting seconds of *Schnapps*.

We were four in the house. The eldest had moved out by then and I had her room. Every morning at six o'clock, the son, an apprentice at his father's (and my) employer, would wake me up with a loud fist-knock, bellowing *"Aufstehen!"* (Up-stand!). My vivid seconds-long morning dreams in between the knock and my full attention were of foxholes and smoking rubble, cowering from the *Wehrmacht*. Stefan of the pounding fist was a sullen twenty-something, with a wispy moustache and glowering stare. He never said much. In the commute to work in his father's BMW that sped along the *Autobahn* to Mannheim at 100 miles an hour, windows sealed to the air-conditioning, as Herr G.'s cigarillos enveloped us in a day-long stink, we were uniformly quiet.

I was terrible at office tasks. I overthought them, I played a manic defensive game, and my German wasn't all that good. My most famous mistake involved being asked to copy a list of steel shapes, mechanical drawings of which were kept in a book that was so overflowing with pages, it looked like a water-logged telephone book, fanning out to the point where you couldn't see its spine. I didn't realize that there was a clip that held the pages together, and thus a way to remove these pages, which might have led me to take a different approach to my task that morning. After an hour of laboriously riffling through the book, identifying and listing the shapes by their catalogue number, then copying their shape with as steady a hand as I could next to their corresponding number, my supervisor, Fräulein M. came over to my folding table and demanded to know what I was doing. Translated for your convenience was her follow-up statement.

"When I said copy, I meant *photocopy*." Then from across the room, in German I understood perfectly.

"What did she do this time?" Exasperation needs no translation. It was going to be a long summer at the steel firm.

But back in Ketsch, I was a proud member of the tribe. Herr G. had a new audience for his ridiculous German-language jokes...how he loved transliterating the compound nouns for me! As most people know, even the non-German speakers among us, compound nouns in German are a way of life. Did you know that a parachutist in German transliterates as a "fallumbrellajumper?" Herr G. would chuckle uncontrollably over this fact each time, as if for the first time. Compound nouns can make German easy, but they can also make German hard. To wit: *Handschuh?* Glove.

Fingerspitzengefühl? It transliterates as fingertipfeeling but does not mean reading in Braille, nor palpation, nor ticklish. It means tactfulness; go figure. But my all-time favorite, not only for its multiple syllables that I have since mastered, but for its searing meaning, has to be *Vergangenheitsbewältigung.* The coping with a painful past; a word that came into being after the Second World War when the German *Volk* needed some serious deprogramming.

Before *Schnapps* and after the main meal was *Nachtisch*—if you have been paying attention, you remember that *Tisch* means table. *Nach* means after. So dessert transliterates as "aftertable." And after the aftertable was the table tennis, hence my greatest scholarly contribution to the German canon, *Nachtischtennis,* or aftertabletennis.

Stefan of the pounding fist was an even fiercer table tennis player. I considered myself proficient at the game, but this was not evident in our nightly matches. I was lucky to score one point out of 21. Three amounted to a victory. No part of Stefan believed in coddling the guest, and no part of me wanted coddling. The *Schnapps* may have helped my reflexes, but certainly the nightly practice amounted to increasingly keener hand-eye coordination, a surer shot, a harder smash and sometimes as many as seven points by the end of that summer.

Nachtischtennis was a form of redemption for both of us, but particularly for Stefan, whose domination may have been an important part of his own inner work. He seemed to take out all his frustrations of an apprenticeship in a company he did not particularly love, under the shadow of a father for whom he seemed to have mixed feelings, on my paddle, the safest target. For me, *Nachtischtennis* was a metaphor for the extreme conditions under which I was surviving full-immersion language acquisition in an unfamiliar office setting—let alone the family-style meals with gruff factory workers every day at lunchtime—as I saw myself grow in confidence at the *Tischtennis Tisch* and off it. We had built our own tradition, Stefan and I, and as a result I felt a real kinship with my sullen German brother. We even shared a laugh now and again. The same can be said for my relationship with my officemates, Fräulein M. and Frau K. If there isn't a word in German for embracing humiliation *(Demütigungumarmung?),* there should be. It is surely how we grow.

Alma Pater

The greatest honor of my life was to be invited to
address the graduating class of my beloved *alma mater*,
The Foote School, a Kindergarten-through-9th grade
private school in New Haven, Connecticut. I talked to the
graduating class about the countless benefits of alumni
networks, about my own class's bonding over our shared
love of our *alma mater*. I asked the winners of that year's
Latin Prize what *alma mater* meant and they both
shrugged. Look at me, dunking on the ninth graders. I
had only recently googled it myself, but the discovery had
surprised this dogged scholar of romance language. I had
long shared the misguided belief with many that *alma*,
as in the Spanish *alma*, or the French *alme*, referred to
the soul. The Mother Soul. Foote, Choate and Smith
College were indeed mother souls who safely delivered
me my lifelong soulmates. But it turns out *Alma* means
nurturing or nursing. *Alma Mater* = Nursing Mother. I
nursed from the teat of Foote, then Choate, and finally
Smith.

N.B. I have every gas spring that opens up an
American-made hatchback car to thank for my private-
school education. Our father introduced and supplied
this product to all three of the Detroit carmakers back in

the 70s. I fairly stand at attention at the slow salute of a Ford Fiesta hatchback, in homage to Dear Old Dad.

If those schools were my nurturing mothers, then Yale University, the "college" in the college town our parents settled shortly before my birth, Yale would be my *alma pater*.

Yale shows up in practically every ring of the trunk of my life. Yale New Haven Hospital was the site of my first breath. In the 60s Yale's Peabody Museum, with its awe-inspiring collection of dinobilia and other natural wonders, was a go-to for Foote class trips. In the early 70s it was all about the Yale Whale, both for rowdy Yale hockey games as well as for Sunday public skating sessions. We lived at the Yale Whale on Sundays. Some of us had our first make-out sessions in the abandoned, overheated walk-in phone booth on the upper level. I learned to ride a horse at Yale's equestrian center, and how to chisel dry mud out of a horse's hoof, how to rub them down thoroughly, from quarter to fetlock, how to post like English aristocracy and canter like a cowgirl. I learned to sail at the Yale Corinthian Yacht Club where, as a teenager I was force-fed all the terms you could possibly need to avoid dying at sea in a 420 Sailing Dinghy. For example, the term for the rope that controls the main sail (or mainsail, pronounced mainsull, fast), is the mainsheet (who came up with this nonsense?) and you are supposed to let go of it if you "hike out" too far (that means lean out of a tilting boat to right it, as far as you can until your hair is wet or you fall into the heaving drink, as I did). I would not let go of the mainsheet. This was no longer the rope that controlled the boat's speed— it was my lifeline. Yale could be a cruel taskmaster.

An *alma pater* is not the school you attended. An *alma pater* is where you learn some of your greatest life lessons. How to save yourself from drowning in the swells of the Atlantic on just your wits when you are forced to drop the mainsheet. How to clean out a horse stall like Hercules, or you won't be asked back. How to kiss a boy like they do in the movies, wearing hockey skates.

My mother ran the Financial Aid Office at the Yale Divinity School, my second home in the 70s. I would swing by on my bike after school or drop by during school vacations with a new purchase, or to fill her in on the latest gossip. Everyone at Yale who knew her loved my mother. Even our current presiding bishop (America's Archbishop of Canterbury) The Very Reverend Michael Curry, who memorably officiated

Meghan and Harry's Royal Wedding, loved Mom. I ran an infant daycare center one high-school summer at the Divinity School. My sister was down the hall with the preschoolers. I was in their pristine Marquand Chapel one fall Saturday afternoon of my senior year at Smith, maid of honor at the marriage of my former Choate roommate and Foote classmate. When her grandfather (whom I shared for practical purposes) was Sterling Professor of Philosophy at Yale, he proved the existence of God through logic and tried to explain it to me in layman's terms. In a sentence, if you speak of God, whether or not you believe in God, you have just made God real, like it or not. Something like that.

Yale of my early college years was summed up in two words: open bar. Yes, I was enrolled at Smith College, a venerable institution of higher learning exclusively for women or those who identify as such. My sister was a senior at Smith and drove us up and down Interstate 91 for school breaks. As soon as I saw my way clear, I would borrow her car to make the weekly trek home with a soccer teammate who was still dating her high school sweetheart, a swimmer at Yale. We had developed quite a nice rhythm to our week. Take classes, win (some) soccer games, study in the free moments, then buzz down to Yale for a well-deserved break.

A quick hello to the folks, and I would dash off to campus, where my best friends from high school were preparing for another wild weekend of drinking, dancing and vomiting. Surrounded by smart boys and girls, my adopted social scene perfectly enhanced my women's college experience back in Northampton. There were practical upsides to a single-sex education: at Smith, there would be no fighting over funding with the better resourced men's sports teams or extra-curricular clubs. Our classrooms were never overpowered by the opinions of young men finding their voice. (They were instead overpowered by young women doing the same.) My housemates, teammates and classmates would become my lifelong peeps. And yet, in the first weeks and months, I felt a lack that dancing the night away at Yale helped address.

After a night of total debauchery (the drinking age in Connecticut was a mere 18 back then so we weren't breaking any laws), I would body slam the early-morning stench of my friends' triple room, grab my stuff and hit the shower before meeting my father outside of the Freshman Quad, a Hogwarts facsimile still shrouded in darkness and mist, for a ride to indoor mixed doubles. I may have looked and smelled as fresh as a new shampoo, but underneath my bubbly exterior was a crowded pool hall, swirling inside me like a 'flu.

This was my first experience with an indoor court. The still air scented with ball fuzz, the hum of blueish overhead lights, and the pleasantly yielding flooring gave my depleted system an extra boost. Mixed doubles with my dad—this was also a first. I wanted to make him proud of my hustle, my occasional put-away, and especially, my cheery demeanor. He didn't need to know about the gross excesses of the night before, though much of the contents of the previous evening would have been evaporating through my pores during our match, so he may have known more than he ever let on. Friendly, charming, a dependable player with pre-war anglicisms for every occasion, my father was the perfect cure for an erratic, self-conscious, hungover, and, what's the opposite of asset? Debit? Daddy's Little Debit.

But Dad would jolly me along the whole way and I would redouble my efforts to please him, in spite of the poor decisions from the night before. Or because of them.

I had no trouble with a fried breakfast and some late-morning REM sleep before some book-learning and a hasty return to campus for Round Two. The next morning, I would collect my carpool buddy to head back to school. This was the routine. Road trip, booze, doubles, booze, road trip. Repeat.

Your *alma pater* can never actually replace your *alma mater*. Sure, I had my fun stumbling from party to post, but I learned over that fall semester that weekends in New Haven were threatening my ability to excel in the classroom, to build my own community at my own school, and to institute safer behaviors on my weekends "in season." I would come to feel a deep and abiding affiliation with my own college community that would depend on the likes of Yale not at all. But that doesn't mean Yale didn't have a great deal to do with launching the "me" I have ultimately become.

I like to think that as a mere townie who has moved confidently her whole life long through the Yale campus like a raccoon at nightfall, I have taken from my *alma pater* every good thing I have ever learned in his gabled shadows. I treasure some of life's best moments: youth group at Batell Chapel; the Yale Rep's production of Aristophanes' *The Frogs* in the swimming pool at the Payne Whitney Gym; Yale/Harvard games when the Bulldogs won; 13-year-old me tangling with a scruffy middle schooler in a walk-in phone booth in the belly of the Whale; 19-year-old me with my first ponytail wrestling with a handsome goalkeeper in his single bed, or most especially, me as a college freshman of an early fall Saturday, making plays and making memories with my actual *pater*, the man who has had so much to do with my enjoyment of tennis.

Under African Skies

Thanks to the enormous generosity of the parents of my beloved Smith friend, when I lived in London in my 20s, I rented an affordable room in their flat in the most beautiful early 19th century square in Bloomsbury, a brisk walk to the south of King's Cross Station. Virginia and Leonard Woolf had lived in the square before the war, and just down the row of stately frontages and across a narrow road, Charles Dickens had made his home. At the center of the square was a locked garden for residents' use; two leafy acres of winding walkways under enormous plane trees and a tennis court at its center. I met a neighbor, a young banker on secondment from Johannesburg, who lived a few doors down from me, and we made a tennis date. Little did I know how important tennis would become in our story.

Like any good liberal arts college graduate, I had put in my time protesting our college endowment's investment in South Africa's heinous system of *Apartheid*, and I was somewhat hesitant to get to know this tall, handsome oppressor. It turns out I was the one guilty of prejudice in assuming the worst of a white South African. His family was made up exclusively of anti-apartheid activists, who protested, volunteered their time and talent to the cause, and paid fair wages to the locals who had lived and worked for generations on their farm in the Eastern Cape.

The tennis was hot, but our affair was brief, culminating in a romantic week together in Italy before he had to return home. In the subsequent months, we wrote regularly. I was humbled by his thoughtful correspondence; his informed opinions on world affairs, on his country's struggles, on literature, music...he was a deep thinker and a kind soul. Seemingly unrelated to this epistolary love affair, or perhaps because of the frustrations of a long-distance relationship, I caught a wave of depression that took me entirely by surprise and to unfamiliar depths of despair. I gained several pounds in my efforts to quell my hollow angst. As my clothes tightened, my self-esteem deteriorated, and I began to regret having arranged a prolonged Christmas visit to South Africa. Weeks turned into days before I was to leave. I tried to go easy on my English aunt's Christmas pudding as a last resort.

And then I waddled off to Heathrow for the 11-hour flight.

He met me at the Johannesburg airport, strikingly fit and tan compared to my doughy Anglo-Saxon pallor, a tad formal in his greeting. On the drive back to his house in Jo'burg, he confessed to having had a fling that had lasted longer than the time we had physically spent together. He concluded that he didn't see us working out. This was on Day One of a three-week visit. I was 6,000 miles away from everything and everyone who could see me through this shocking setback. Overweight, insecure, and alone in my grief, I saw myself as having two choices. I could give in to the catastrophe of a broken heart, or I could start climbing out of this wretched darkness and enjoy the most exotic trip of my life.

The Republic of South Africa urged me to choose the latter.

Each morning I would strategize another day as a dumped woman trapped on a three-week date. I would cheer myself on with whispered mantras: "It never gets easier; you just get better!" I was a human fridge magnet. It helped that I was in the most beautiful place in the world, for we had left monochromatic Johannesburg for Cape Town: a bright and shiny city nestled around a harbor, dominated by a mountain with its top lopped off. Now imagine fog coming in over the mountain—literally seeping over the top—just like a tablecloth. We hiked Table Mountain on New Year's Eve, and I saw nothing but natural grandeur and the twinkly lights of a cozy civilization. On the other hand, driving past miles of shantytown in and around Cape Town in an endless display of deprivation, or visiting Robben Island, where Nelson Mandela was incarcerated for most of twenty years, felt like a slow beating. I was so affected by my surroundings that I totally lost the capacity to feel sorry for myself. I met all kinds of people, including the mother of my host's best friend, a dearie who had had a complicated entanglement with my best friend back in London, and whose mother never once made eye contact with me. When I complimented her on the delicious lunch she served us, she answered in a sing song, *My black hands!*

On the Garden Route to the Eastern Cape, I took in the native flora like a dog with her head out of the window. Not one bloom, nor tangy scent was recognizable. We visited charming colonial towns and listened to books on tape on long, empty roads dotted with *rondavels,* round huts with grass rooves and slots for windows. The weight I had gained in cold, drizzly England melted away under the summer sun of the Southern Hemisphere. We played that game-with-the-wooden-paddles-and-squishy-ball on a beach on the

Wild Coast. I remember counting up to well over 100 hits without a single mistake between us, no longer a sign that we were destined to be together for life. When we arrived at his family farm, I met his welcoming parents, his three friendly brothers and their bubbly teenage sister. If they only knew what heartache had accompanied me there!

As with the initial *coup de foudre* of our affair in London, I found a safe and comfortable place on this happy farm. We took the horses out for long rides that never reached the edges of their vast property that bordered the Kingdom of Lesotho, we swam in watering holes, visited with neighbors, read in the garden, ate fresh food, traded stories and laughed until we choked. I danced with the locals, worshipped in their Anglican church...I was enthralled by the native tongue, *Xhosa*, with its clicks and murmurs and whoops. I was filled to overflowing with exotica, from the first note of the dawn chorus to the last cluster of stars in that unfamiliar night sky.

His mother was surprised to learn in a quiet tête-à-tête that this cheerful Yank with the beaming smile and a perpetual spring in her step was no longer romantically involved with her son. We talked as women do, from the heart. She assured me that her eldest was someone who took his time with things, someone who felt deeply but loved cautiously. I was quite the opposite. I had fallen in love with this rambunctious family, these people, and their ways.

Nearly every afternoon, sometimes long into the evening, the family played tennis. Their father had built the court, and it was the center of family life. So much tennis! Energetic, playfully competitive doubles with a rotation of jolly partners, hard-charging singles among the men...this was where my former boyfriend was in his element. And it was on that court, lustily swinging racquets and scrambling for tough shots, where he rediscovered his connection with me, to that long ago date on the court in our London square. In the safety of those painted lines, in the predictable scoring of games and sets, he relaxed at last into the realization that he *did* want to make a go of things. He *did* want me to move from London to Johannesburg, to get my own place, my own job, so that we could try again, in earnest. But by then, it was too late. I had rediscovered joy—the kind you carry around with you, that isn't tied to happily-ever-afters, or others' opinions of you—a joy so all-encompassing, so untainted—I knew for certain that his cautious heart simply would never be able to keep pace.

Postscript: I am friends on Facebook-er-Meta with his brother, who often posts stunning photos of the farm, now run by their younger brother. One photo hit me so hard I nearly fell over from the weight of loss: it was a picture of the first structure his parents had built as newlyweds, a sort of shed where they slept until the farmhouse was built...a shed next to "where the tennis court used to be," now completely overrun with native grass. "Used to be?" No! It is still there! That hallowed half acre is nothing short of a spiritual vortex! All the passion expressed on that court...all the intense focus and lighthearted camaraderie...all of it has seeded that wild grass, there under African skies.

A Gentlemen's Club

I remember a lecture in college on media literacy, how the powers of persuasion in advertising were honed by rigorous psychological research. For example, the brain registers when something isn't right, quite subconsciously, and pays better attention as a result. In the case of a particularly compelling advertisement, the lecturer showed us a zoomed-in photo of an ice cube in a tempting glass of some name-brand beverage and there scrawled in the contours of the ice was the f-word. Apparently, our brains registered that word subliminally, and the science showed that such an aberration made us pause for longer than otherwise, to process this sneaky neurological ambush. The theory went that this pause would give us enough time to create a relationship, however brief, with the beverage. I concluded from this revolutionary knowledge that the very same part of the brain that can read a swear word in an ice cube is activated when things go down that just don't feel right. And we need to listen for that activation.

So it was in the basement of one of the grandest gentlemen's clubs in London, built in 1847, whose former members include luminaries such as Tennyson, Thackeray, and Trollope, sundry dukes and viscounts and some 57 Nobel Laureates, where I was treated to a game of squash with a retired colonel I had met, I have absolutely no idea when, or where. This was over thirty years ago, when I was a swinging singleton with a British passport thanks to Dear Old Dad, and I was in a near constant state of adventure. Somewhere along the way, I had met an elderly former military officer who liked to play squash and I was invited to play at his club. No doubt I rolled up on my bicycle; my flat in Bloomsbury was no distance from Pall Mall. We made our way down to the basement, to a squash court not unlike the ones the British built across India during the days of the Raj, a musty wooden box with tight seams and dust in the corners, that opened onto a corridor across from 'his and hers' dressing rooms. I was shown to the 'hers,' where I changed into my kit.

When I met the colonel on the lacquered court, the knobby-kneed old geezer in the fluttering shorts knelt in front of my plimsolls (ah, the quaint vocabulary of my 20s in London, when sweaters were jumpers and sneakers were plimsolls and whatever you put on for sport was your kit) and asked me if I wanted him to check my feet. He claimed to be a trained podiatrist. There was something about his barely concealed breathlessness that gave me pause. Had my head been under an MRI, that patch of grey matter that can read ice cubes would have been lighting up like Regent Street at Christmastime. I demurred politely and we went on with the game. I remember beating him as gently as I could, being a third his age and the better player. When it was all over, and I was a pinker, moister version of myself, he asked me again if I would like him to check my feet. I would not. I had heard about foot fetishes, assumed they were more legend than fact. This felt like fact. My answer sounded breezy enough, to mask my distinct discomfort at being gang-pressed into removing my shoes.

Granted, had I had an appointment at his alleged podiatry office, I would have kicked off my plimsolls with abandon, but I dare say in that lone squash court in the bowels of one of London's grandest clubs, I doubted entirely the colonel's qualifications and intentions. You might wonder what the harm would be in showing an old man my sweaty feet, and my answer would be that nothing at that moment could have felt creepier. Creepy and yet familiar; I can remember describing to my big brother when we were in our teens that dating boys at that age made me feel like territory under siege. They advanced across my terrain like an invading army, and I found myself helplessly surrendering borders as I fought to protect the interior.

We made our way into our separate changing rooms, and it was then that I realized that my door didn't lock. In fact, it swung into the room invitingly. My ice-cube reader was jangling as I scanned the airless room for a blockade. This took the form of a four-foot-tall fire extinguisher which I dragged up against the door before stripping out of my stinky clothes for a quick shower. It was precisely at that moment, between the stripping and the shower, that the door flew open, all of half an inch, where it met the fire extinguisher with a loud report.

"Oh Miss Bigwood," the old colonel bleated with a trembling voice, "are you sure you don't want me to inspect your feet?"

I sometimes wonder what would have happened had I not barricaded myself in the ladies' room that afternoon. Clearly, my intruder would have had no chance of overwhelming this young, athletic soccer goalkeeper but I would not have savored the encounter, stark naked with all ten toes exposed. What the podiatrist would not have anticipated is that along with my British passport, I also inherited my father's wide, stubby-toed feet. *Peasant feet*, as my Swedish friend describes her equally mannish dogs. *Plates of meat*, in Cockney Rhyming Slang. He would have been sorely disappointed. But the real takeaway from my adventure in the basement of the gentlemen's club in Pall Mall: don't wait for an MRI to be told what you already know. And as for the breeziness, I recommend something gustier.

Ball Boy

You are six years old. You have lost both your parents. You live with other orphans and children whose parents have been sent to work in the Killing Fields. In your only pair of shorts, you labor daily from dawn to dusk harvesting rice in the paddies. It is a never-ending cycle of work, songs about the motherland and your leader Pol Pot, with never enough food, nor rest. Years pass this way. One day your older sister and her husband tell you that you are leaving here with a group of strangers. You are all going to walk to the border—it will take weeks. She gives you a baby pig as a pet. It is the only joy in your lonely life. You carry it on the walk, until you cannot. You and the pig must be very careful not to step on land mines along the way. If you see food on the road, or clothing, you must fight every instinct not to run to it. Treats are most likely wired to explode.

"Tell your little brother that tonight we roast the pig." You are inconsolable.

Your sister must help you walk: your feet are too heavy, your arms, empty, your heart, broken. Eventually, you reach the Thai border. You find yourselves in a crowded refugee camp, but there is food, and you find a new pet, a hen! Your hen lays eggs! You sell them at the border and that buys you a few small comforts; more food, a sense of purpose. Your sister's belly is growing with a child inside. But something is growing on your neck. Something ugly and puffy that makes people stare. One person who stares up close is a Red Cross worker, who recognizes that you have cervical tuberculous lymphadenitis, commonly known as scrofula. The Red Cross wants to take you to America to fix you. You may bring your sister, her husband and their baby. First, they fly you to the Philippines, where you must wait until they are ready to put you on a plane to New York. This refugee camp is surrounded by mountains and streams. There is more to eat. You sleep in sheets and dream of flying, close to the ground, with a swimming motion.

One morning in Manila, on your way to collecting your medicine, you come upon four Red Cross doctors playing a game with sticks with nets hitting a ball back and forth. They see you watching them and offer to pay you a few *centavos* to chase the balls for them. The balls go everywhere. You say to yourself, *I could play this game.*

A nice lady and her husband meet your young family at the airport in New York. They are so tall, and their smiles are of people with full bellies. In the car ride you smell fruit and flowers as the lady lulls you to sleep, quietly reading the exit signs in your ear as your nephew fusses in the back. She is teaching you to count in English.

They have an apartment for your little family. You sleep on the couch and the baby sleeps in the bed with your sister and her husband. You go to school and sit in class with much younger children. At home you don't get enough to eat. You miss your mother, who loved you like a favorite doll. You miss your father, who one day collected wood, drew water, dressed in his best shirt and pants, went to sleep and never woke up. You miss the house on stilts where you were safe from crawling things and high water. Now you are living with noise above you, to each side, even below you. But the noise in the next room is the worst. Baby crying, which shouting makes worse, and angry whispers from your sister who once sang to you. The next time the nice old lady visits the apartment, the baby is still crying, your brother-in-law is in one of his dark moods. Your tired sister glares at you to go play in the bedroom.

The lady decides then and there to bring you home to live with her and her old husband in their big house. The nice lady had no intention of having an 11-year-old Cambodian boy come live with them, but she is firm.

The old man agrees, but only if you call them Grandmother and Grandfather. He has successfully raised and launched four young adults. He is in no way up for a fifth. You pick their flowers and make beautiful bouquets in thanks. That first summer, the lady takes you to a municipal day camp, to keep you busy while she is at work. They teach you the game with the sticks and nets. It is called tennis. Just as you had thought, when you hit the balls, they don't go everywhere. They go where you want them to go. At home, you hit the ball against the garage door every day until it is time for dinner. Five years later, you play Number One Singles on your high school team. You string other people's racquets for pocket money. You are recruited by a college for your tennis prowess. You are given a full ride, because even though you live with people of some means, you have never been adopted. This was purposeful, for even though you are a member of the family in every sense, as a refugee, you are penniless when you apply to schools.

You play tennis and soccer in college, and they call you by your American name. You go on to earn master's degrees in business and finance. Today, you are a grey-haired banker in Boston. You are a USPTA coach and teach tennis on the weekends to the underprivileged. My Cambodian brother whom I have never called by your American name.

Over the years, when I have been anxious about this or that, you have reassured me that nothing can ever be as bad as dodging landmines on a long walk to the border. You have also taught me that everyone, no matter what their background or circumstances, deserves a fair shot. Even an orphan from Cambodia with a swollen neck and one pair of shorts. Especially him.

That's What Fathers Are For!

How to describe my father? He was as gentle and kind as any grandfather, with laugh lines that crisscrossed his temples, yet when I was growing up, he had the scariest yelling voice I had ever heard from man or beast. He couldn't get through a story without chortling uncontrollably, and he was the only member of our family who wept at movies. He was tall and handsome, and a very humble small businessman. He was British, with a Belgian accent. As the youngest of four, and after having been subjected more than once to his roars of frustration, I made it my mission in life to never, ever, upset this truly dear man.

This meant saying yes to every trip to the hardware store if he wanted company, taking long hikes, just the two of us, that ended with hot chocolate at the local dairy bar, even though I didn't particularly like hot chocolate back then (why would you pour a mug of hot water over a chocolate bar and serve it? I preferred my chocolate unwrapped), encouraging him to tell a funny story he had told a dozen times before...when Dad was in a good mood, the planet spun giddily.

When my mother happened upon Dear Old Dad (I imagine her on the streets of post-war Brussels sweeping an oversized metal detector, but for husbands), it would have been akin to finding that favorite glove you thought you'd lost. The story goes she proposed after three weeks. In fact, he professed his love for her, to which she responded,

"What are you going to do about it?"

"Marry you?"

The sophisticated American dame working for the State Department, starring in a local English-language amateur theatre production of *The Heiress*, knew for certain the sweet, innocent (I really should capitalize that word) stagehand who had grown up in Brussels as the middle child of English ex-pats, who fled with his family on May 10, 1940 when the Germans rolled into town, only to be relocated to a motherland where he had never actually lived, now back in Brussels with his Civil Engineering degree, was her ticket to Happily Ever After. (That was one sentence.)

They raised us in the States (except for that trial year in Brussels when we kids were five, seven, nine and eleven, and we forced him to move us back at ages six, eight, ten and twelve). Back in New Haven, we rented houses from professors on sabbatical until we could buy one for a family of six. Early on, Dad built us a table tennis table out of plywood, which we set up on sawhorses in whichever driveway it happened to be whichever summer. At seven, I sat impatiently on the sideline, waiting for my big brother to finish his games with Dad so I could have my first.

After every errant shot Peter would crack *Sorry about that, chief*, a quote from his favorite TV show. Dad of infinite patience (unless you did something criminal) finally interrupted,

"That's enough now."

It occurs to me that he yelled so long and loud when pushed to the brink because we four drove him stark-raving mad.

Finally, it was my turn to play. It was one thing to fool around at the game with my siblings. It was quite another to face my father on the other side of the net. I had waited my entire life for this moment. My arms could barely clear the table for my pathetic serves. I scraped my tender skin on dad's homemade edges in an effort to return his loopy volleys. I was overly warm and out of breath. I stumbled after the balls that eluded me and paused for rests at every opportunity. It took forever for my father to reach twenty-one, yet I am sure he beat me handily. When he offered to play another game, I reluctantly refused. Inside, I went straight into my mother's arms, sobbing. She felt my forehead and ran for the thermometer. It turns out I had a temperature of 103.

That was the first of hundreds of games. Whenever Dad won, which was pretty much all the time, he would point out that *That's what fathers are for!* Whenever I suggested a game, he would say *Why, do you want to get trounced?* or, *Do you want to get beaten by your father?* If good parenting involves consistency, my father was a great parent. To this day, I can hear his teasing tone:

"The object of the exercise is to hit the ball *over* the net!"

When Dad got t-boned by Alzheimer's, the last thing to go was the table tennis. Into his eighties, he could only manage a couple of games, but he could keep score better than I could. It was as if everything else in his world had shut down except for keeping score at table tennis. Let's say I slammed one that ended up in the bushes (we still played in the driveway, only now it was my driveway), he could go off to find it, come back, and still know the score. It was frankly miraculous. I couldn't even do that. I had so much on my mind—divorce proceedings, overseeing the care of two sick parents, raising two larger-than-life kids (it's genetic), meeting a million obligations with very little strategy...I would forget the score, who was serving, even what day of the week it was. Not Dad. His tenacity was hard won, but it was impressive. I used to think *this must be what living in the present looks like*. I could place the ball and return most shots by then, so I admit to winning most of our games at the end of an old man's life. But by the time we were done and had put away the paddles and ball and were heading inside for a glass of *ginger pop*, it was all a mirage.

"One of these days I'll beat you, Dad. But not today!"

"That's what fathers are for!"

Taxonomy of Tennis

Scoter (n) /ˈskōdər/

1.   a northern diving duck that winters off the coast, the male of which has mainly black plumage.

2.   an elderly male of the species *Homo Sapiens*, predominantly of the Caucasian variety that swings a tennis racquet and parades his innate privilege in the form of dour sanctimony, mainly targeted at younger females of the species.

3.   my first husband.

My first husband and I had a shared love of tennis. One of our first dates was on a tennis court, where our long rallies apparently expressed sexual tension though I was entirely unaware of this fact. I spent that fateful match simply trying to return his low whistlers from my baseline. This misreading of the unspoken should have been a tell that we were not destined for lifelong compatibility. I would venture to add that this 'sexual tension' morphed into more of an abiding disappointment over the next fifteen years and we ultimately agreed, through largely uncontentious mediation, to part ways.

There were some great times, no denying it, because we shared compatible senses of humor, not to mention truly enchanting children. I wouldn't trade in that first husband for anything because I learned a lot from him about sacrifice (mine) and I would never give back those kids.

One of the enduring areas of mutual enjoyment apart from tennis is the vocabulary we made up, or dusted off from my childhood, whence an endless stream of made-up terms originated. (An unrecognized claim to fame: my sister and I coined "peeps" in the 1970s.) One marriage counselor suggested that even though my first husband rarely declared his love for me, he showed me that love by riffing on that which made me laugh, including those terms unique to my family of origin. I honestly appreciated this about the old coot.

Which brings me to the scoter. We read about scoters after a particularly productive day on a small lake in Northern California we would visit when we were dating. We would take a canoe out and chase coots around the lake to see them peel off with effortful paddling across the water's surface. It was a fine pastime at the gloaming, after a cocktail and before a late summer dinner.

Coots are not ducks. They are more closely related to the Sandhill Crane than to their web-toed proximates.

In our research about the coot, we discovered the scoter, another species of waterfowl easily confused for the coot. Linguistically speaking, discovering the scoter was like happening upon oil in the back forty. As if to a starting gun, we promptly incorporated scoter into our household vernacular. We reasoned that if old men could be coots, then cranky old men could be scoters. In no time, the noun assumed the highest status; that of the verb. I can still hear my ex-husband:

"I'm going to scote, hon...you have to wash the sharp knives right after you use them."

When I mentioned The Common Scoter to my friend the editor-in-chief of a well-known blog, we engaged in some serious contextualizing (which is why we are such good friends). What is a scoter's essence? What makes a scoter tick? Where are they found in captivity? She and I were primarily tennis friends in the very early days of our thirty-year friendship. One day, we were running each other around in a friendly rally when two latter-day septuagenarians showed up at the gate to the fenced-in public court.

"Did you girls sign up for this court?" one of them croaked. What they meant by "sign up," was to twirl the dials on cast-iron clock mock-ups, to signal when we were starting and when we were finishing. We had not. We didn't yet know about this sign-in procedure as we were new to this court. And we explained as much. They didn't care. Our rally ended with a whimper as the two men took over the court. They didn't so much as give us a sheepish 'better-luck-next-time' shrug. They simply took the castle.

"Are they scoters?" my friend whispered as we slunk off. These were, indeed, scoters. Domesticated scoters have more pronounced attributes than those found in the wild and are more easily genotyped. If a scoter comes to visit you by car, the very first topic of conversation will inevitably be about the traffic getting there. Once traffic patterns have been covered in their entirety, scoters will move on to weather. In fact, any time you need to lull a scoter into submission, turn on the Weather Channel. They will be transfixed for the duration. Scoters walk into a newly decorated room and notice the paint drip on a windowpane. Scoters sing Happy Birthday out of key, loudly. Scoters snore and claim they don't. Scoters on the tennis court double as linesmen, for both sides.

I was once assigned a scoter as a mixed-doubles partner. Turns out I had a lot to learn about the game of tennis! I wasn't rushing the net nearly enough, my volley grip was wrong, I was putting too much weight on my heels, I wasn't calling balls, I wasn't calling plays...apparently, I wasn't even poaching enough! At the end of the match, I felt like I should have handed him a check. It got worse in the clubhouse afterwards. I wasn't just this old guy's tennis partner; I was a stand-in for his late wife. He steered me through doorways like a ballroom dancer and invaded my air space like a bombing mission, with stories from his illustrious past. I don't even remember who else was at the table because I never heard from any of them. Scoters have a way of monopolizing entire afternoons. They know in their heart of hearts that no one within pontificating distance can speak over their throaty calls.

One widow of a scoter told me that on their first (and last!) cruise, they had to find a new dinner table every evening because after a night listening to her late husband regale them with his experiences in well-heeled Washington D.C., no one wanted them back. My first husband wasn't this kind of scoter. He was what he and I affectionately called a scoter-in-training. When I was married to him, he cared a great deal about traffic patterns and weather, and the most excited he ever got was when describing someone else's driving infraction. He could scote with the best of them, but he still has a long way to go before he earns his wings. The White-Winged Scoter, on the other hand, is the apex of the Class Aves, and he has made his way to my new tennis club 3,000 miles from where we first discovered scoters in the wild.

Just the other day, my daughter and I were sharing the ball machine as we do most mornings (she is obsessed with her new sport, and I am obsessed with her); three minutes on, then switch, as in a relay race. This is a great way to 'play with a beginner'— she hits her shots and I hit mine. We both sweat and grow. She was in the middle of her three-minute session when the door to the lobby swung open and two older gentlemen appeared courtside. It is impossible to reach the second court on this side of the lobby without either skirting half the length of the first court (our court on this occasion) ducking behind the curtain at the back and reappearing at the other end of the building at the far side of the second court. Or, if the people playing on the first court offer, you can dart straight across, along the net, and pass through the curtain dividing the two courts.

These two gentlemen in tennis whites came upon my daughter dashing back and forth at the baseline, in something approximating a mad frenzy. They could see with a trained eye that her opponent was a ball machine, relentlessly launching tough backhands, alternating with tougher cross-court forehands. And yet they waited. They stood in silence and waited. What were these White Wing Scoters waiting for? For the heaping ball machine to empty itself before they took the shortcut, bisecting our court? That would have taken twenty minutes. Were they waiting for my daughter to interrupt her workout, trot over to the other side of the court and pause the machine? Or were they Korean War vets frozen in place, reliving an artillery ambush?

Finally, they wandered down the alley toward the ball machine and rather than duck behind the safety of the curtain, staggered along the baseline behind the machine, cringing and wincing and dodging the balls my daughter was hitting with increasing ferocity. The upside to their intrusion? I have never seen my daughter play better.

We are still wondering what they were waiting for. Honestly, I am just waiting for their extinction.

Come On, Now

Palo Alto, California isn't just an overpriced leafy enclave housing Silicon Valley's movers and shakers living cheek-by-jowl in uniform opulence. It is in its own right a hive of technological wizardry. Palo Alto is where Mr. Hewlett met Mr. Packard, where Stanford University cranks out patents and Nobel prize winners like widgets, where nearby Google chose to have its dazzling main campus, where Facebook-er-Meta set up shop and where just down El Camino Real, Tesla launched their eponymous electric vehicles.

If Palo Alto were an actual hive, its youth would all be queens, fed a steady diet of Royal Jelly. A quick lesson in apiology: in a typical beehive, all larvae are fed the same foodstuff, commonly known as Royal Jelly. After three days, though, workers and drones are cut off from the supply, and the rest is stored in special cells reserved for the young queens. They are fed copious amounts of Royal Jelly, a blockbuster combination of protein, sugars and fatty acids, and therewith develop amazing reproductive organs, unlike their sterile underlings.

They reproduce better, stronger worker bees, drones, and more queens and the cycle repeats *ad infinitum*, or until humans do so much damage to the environment that the bees can't get the sustenance they need to reproduce anymore.

In Palo Alto, the "Royal Jelly" fed our budding aristocrats is made up exclusively of money and connections (not to mention great dollops of parental involvement). By way of example, when my son was a Cub Scout and participated in Pinewood Derbies, in which the scouts design and produce miniature cars from a kit consisting of blocks of pine, plastic wheels and wee metal axles, the timed races would be overseen by Tesla engineers. When they held their bake-off (cakes made by the scouts at home, and judged at the pack meeting), the head judge hailed from the kitchen of the nearby Four Seasons Hotel. Welcome to the hive.

Even the adults get their share of the Royal Jelly. When we undertook to raise funds for academic enrichment, for example (glass-blowing class at the high school doesn't pay for itself, people). At one school fundraiser, I ponied up my $40 for a place in a Round Robin tournament at one of the elite tennis and swimming clubs in town. What made this friendly tournament extra special was that one of the co-hosts was a Wimbledon doubles champion from the 80s.

Twelve lucky mommies in our finest tennis duds showed up for the most exciting tennis of our lives. The Wimbledon champion floated from one court to the next, playing short sets with each of us so that everyone got a chance to play with her, and to play against her. Her metronomic warm-up routine was something to behold. A spring in her tennis shoes seemed battery-powered, and her form was so well honed, you allowed yourself to stare. She was all precision. She weaponized consistency for most of the points that day, all of it executed with grace. (Shy smiles and champions is a lovely combination.) I will never forget the moment one of my assigned partners, a dentist with an erratic swing, hit a low whistler down the alley, passing the Wimbledon champion who was playing net against us. The dentist turned to me, flushed with victory, and whispered *I want to call my husband!*

The Wimbledon champ and I already enjoyed a bond—I was teaching Spanish at her house after school that year to a bunch of fourth graders, including her daughter. We shared laughs about our kids, about other people's kids, about our school...I enjoyed landing punchlines in her presence; her face lit up like a merry-go-round when she laughed. When she was lost in her own thoughts though, walking to or from our kids' school, she tended to pull down the shades, so to speak, and keep to herself. I have always preferred a light-hearted rapport, in our case occasionally punctuated by her handing me cash for my language services, which was honestly a bit embarrassing. But what was I supposed to do? Make these kids memorize Pablo Neruda for free?

On the court, there were no light-hearted moments. For all intents and purposes, this was a Wimbledon reenactment and I formed part of her doubles team. When I made an unforced error, she didn't reassure, nor cosset. She didn't even look me in the eye. She would jog in place, adjust her grip, and in a low voice, clearly directed at me, she would murmur *Come on, now.* Ushered forth through a clenched jaw, under a flinty stare now fixed on our opponents, *come on, now* was for my ears alone, and had the blood-pumping effect of a glorious battle cry.

It was the way she said *come on now* that I have never forgotten. It was all muscle. If that phrase had been an animal, it would have been a puma, slinking along a branch, stalking its prey. This wasn't fun-in-the-sun bandy-about tennis.

And here's where *court étique* comes in; it requires you to learn the fine distinctions that inform the tone of every single match you'll ever play. Some games are all about the repartee and budding friendships. Some are solemn and respectful. League matches can be painfully competitive and no fun whatsoever. This game with my very own Wimbledon champion was like no other ever. It was all business, with none of the noise of quacking self-confidence, nor the immaturity of snobby ladies who need to beat you to justify their expensive lessons, clinics and cute matching outfits. That day we were as one, looking up to someone who had earned our heartfelt admiration and respect. To this day, I use *Come on, now* in my own head, after every mistake. It says *you can do better. A Wimbledon champion told you so.*

For forty dollars' worth of curricular enhancement, *come on, now* woke me up to a truth about sports at any age and in any context that changed me. However friendly a tennis round robin with a bunch of mommies may be, however good-natured I may be off the court, however clever the comebacks on the court with a foursome of friends, tennis is serious, serious business. Sport is serious. Technical excellence, focus, stamina and a winning attitude should not be sacrificed for a jolly good time. That can wait for after the tournament. There is a time and a place for levity. A time and place for making friends and making allowances. But if you are keeping score, the game demands your full attention. That's what *Come on, now* means to me. Bring your whole self. Afterwards, we will laugh.

Almost

After leaving a marriage that made both of us feel underappreciated and overburdened, I got straight to work finding a new life partner. My greatest fear was that my kids would one day have phone conversations that would go something like this:

> *Hey.*
>
> *Hi.*
>
> *You taking Mom this year?*
>
> *Can you take her?*
>
> *I mean probably. Why can't you?*
>
> *We had her at Easter.*
>
> *True.*
>
> *Look, take her for Thanksgiving and we'll do Christmas.*
>
> *You sure you don't mind? Don't you have your in-laws this year?*
>
> *It's fine. We'll make it work.*

This was the scenario that haunted me. Never mind that statistically men die before women, and people die accidentally, and there may ultimately be no avoiding my late-onset spinsterhood, but I wanted to give it my best shot. Furthermore, I longed for a dinner companion through the twilight years. Bonus points for a tennis partner. And if I could wind up this project before my mother with her cancer diagnosis, and Dad with his still manageable Alzheimer's, shuffled off this mortal coil, all the better. I dearly wanted their blessing on my next union.

Early on in my post-divorce dating adventures, I came across someone truly spectacular. Apart from being *funnyandsmart* (Number one requisite), he had retired early from Silicon Valley and led a groovy life of early adoption, seemingly devoid of stress. He drove an electric vehicle (this was pre-Tesla, when EVs were quite uncommon). From the eaves of his painted porch in one of the leafiest streets in Old Palo Alto hung Tibetan prayer flags, before everyone started hanging them. He volunteered his time to causes as far away as Africa and Nepal. And boy, did he love his kids. I have met a few guys like Mr. EV through online dating in Silicon Valley. No matter what their status—single and looking to remarry, single and looking to mingle, newly single, so single you better know some karate—they uniformly indulged their kids. However tough the divorce had been on them (according to a local financial planner, the average "family support" settlement in those parts was a whopping $17,000 a month for a non-celebrity, middle-of-the-road Silicon Valley break up), these resourced daddies spared no post-divorce expense when it came to their spawn. They took them to the Galapagos for Spring Break. Hiking and skiing in the Pyrenees. Trips to NYC to see Broadway shows for the child interested in theatre. They weren't called Disneyland Dads for nothing. But to the passerby on a coffee date, whose earning power afforded no such luxuries and might never again, the view was breathtaking.

This guy was everything you could want in a second husband. He even owned a maple stand in New Hampshire; someone living on the property tapped the trees and bottled the syrup for him. He gave me a bottle and I practically built a shrine for it in my kitchen cupboard.

This international social justice warrior with the Tibetan prayer flags was the Rémy Martin of the in-town bachelors (there were plenty of eccentric power players on the San Francisco Peninsula, but not within bicycling distance) and you didn't waste that stuff on just anybody. Truth to be told, he was simply too rich for my digestion. Even his favorite chocolate, in which he insisted on at least 90% cacao, was lost on me; it tasted like cigar stubs. He told me once about his open-door policy at home, whereby his kids would wander into his bedroom as he and a casual lover were just waking up. Maybe the dark chocolate and bedroom door policy were scare tactics, to weed out the lightweights. If so, they worked.

I had recently damaged my rotator cuff, most acutely felt when reaching for my serve toss, and I had been restricted from tennis until my shoulder healed. It would turn out that squash was the ideal replacement sport—no overhead smashes in my repertoire—and guess who belonged to the tony tennis, squash and swim club that would later be the site of a broken engagement (but that's another tale)?

Thanks to my first-ever sweetheart back in middle school, I had learned to play squash and had kept it up in college with a different sweetheart. Even though I would never be waking up with Mr. EV and his young family, if I gave him a good game, he would keep me around for the squash. (Not to overstate it, but I would choose a rousing game of squash every time over tangling naked with a near stranger in an unsavory dating ritual often involving nose hair or toe fungus, any day of the year.) He would pick me up in my humble rental near the train tracks and whisk me off to his club, where he had an infinite number of guest passes. Our squash was hard core. We played grinding games, point traded for point, game upon game, grunting and sweating, cursing and occasionally colliding, slippery and breathless. It was the height of intimacy without any of the complications.

It went on long after my shoulder had healed, and I was back to my tennis. It lasted through our respective dating adventures and disasters, until about the time I met a guy *who also belonged to that club*, who wanted to marry me, and that is when the squash stopped for good.

Driving home from one of our exhilarating matches, I imagined we were driving home from *our* club, with happily blended young families, reducing our carbon footprint for the good of the planet in our trusty EV. Healing broken parts of ourselves that past relationships had scarred, sharing our deepest desires and our greatest terrors, caring for one another without condition, improving our squash, and maybe he would even pick up tennis. In the silence only an electric vehicle whipping down the highway can muster; he punctured my iridescent daydream.

"I have a date tonight with a professor from Berkeley."

I resumed the role of platonic squash buddy in time to hear all about her online profile. With her multiple degrees, her wide-ranging hobbies and numerous areas of interest and expertise, she made my online profile look like a fast-food menu. She was eminently more his speed. I tried not to feel like too much of a loser—after all, I had won a couple of games that day, shouldn't that count for something? And I already knew that he and I were not meant to be. But a girl can daydream, can't she?

Anyone who has traveled University Avenue toward downtown Palo Alto from Highway 101, has likely noticed Squire House. John Adams (yes, that Adams) Squire, heir to a meat-packing fortune, was a professor at nearby Stanford University at the turn of the 20th century. His 7,000 square-foot mansion was designed by a renowned San Francisco architect in Classic Roman Revival and looks like an antebellum stage set, with porch and portico, complete with sky-high white columns made from Redwood trunks, yet surreally approached by a parade of soaring palm trees. Squire House is Palo Alto in a nutshell, where the coasts clash in colloquial excesses.

As we passed Squire House, Mr. EV remarked, with his typical nonchalance,

"I almost bought that house."

"Well," thought I, without skipping a beat, "in the spirit of anything we don't do becoming something we almost did, I almost married you."

Now I live with a *smartandfunny* man with whom I relocated to New Hampshire, and who announced last winter that he intended to tap our maple trees. I singlehandedly and with great fanfare produced one of the pints of those gallons of maple syrup our trees produced. We have something of a shrine in our cupboard made up of mason jars filled with the sticky nectar. It turns out I didn't want to marry the man who almost bought Squire House. I think I just really wanted a maple stand.

We Got a Runner!

It shouldn't have surprised me that I would meet so many athletes in Northern California, after most of a decade in smoky, boozy, overcast London where fit, tan six-footers were not a thing. Early on in my single-motherhood, I met a soccer goalkeeper just as I had once been, and a tennis player! He was fun, and successful, and incredibly kind. I especially wanted kind. When my mother met him, she opined that *he fit in our family like a gear*. I found a keeper (*double entendre*)! And in the nick of time. My mother was reaching the end of her life and seeing me 'settled' as she put it, meant everything. Amazingly, my beau belonged to the same club where I had played all that squash, and I was back there once again, only this time on the tennis courts and in the swimming pools and at the beautiful restaurant for Mother's Day brunch with my kids. (He didn't have any, which suited mine fine.) We were playing at being a happy family, where people assumed he was the dad, which thrilled him. He spoiled all of us. We loved the attention. We played badminton in the front yard with the kids. It was rollicking good fun, but when I asked my daughter what she thought of him as a boyfriend for her momma, she allowed that he was "very loud." I didn't bother to point out that we are, too. She deserved a voice in this new adventure.

He signed us up for a friendly mixed-doubles tennis tournament at the club. The tennis pro announced the rules, informing us that he had nice new bouncy balls for us. Well, that set my partner off in a way that had hitherto evaded me: he had an enthusiasm for bouncy balls jokes. New balls. Fuzzy balls. Lost balls, your balls, my balls. Not to mention the fact that he kissed me after every point. Ran into my arms after games. Crowed and twirled me when we won sets. It was nauseating. And still with the balls jokes. Never one for confrontation, I simply sidestepped my growing concerns about a grown man who could act such a clown. But I figured over time I could influence him. That was my best strategy. Show him a better way by modeling the desired behavior with the decorousness of Emily Dickinson. This wasn't going to work. (I've since concluded that most grown men have done all their self-civilizing by the time they put down the Beer Pong paddles.)

There are certain things you can't unlearn, and an individual's sense of humor is definitely one of them. I found myself not telling him about invitations I had received, so that I didn't risk him making the equivalent of balls jokes in front of people whose opinion mattered. Lamentably, this enthusiastic lover with stars in his eyes had already asked me to marry him, and I had accepted, in view of the mortal coil and my mother's gear simile. But then came the evening that we were at the club playing singles after work. When he missed a shot, he would howl. I would shudder and carry on. When I passed him with a winning shot, he took his racquet and flung it against the back wall. The contact echoed emphatically in the half-empty hall. Even he looked surprised.

I was raised on John McEnroe throwing his on-court tantrums, and closer to home, a younger version, who played on our club's tennis team, a kid with exceptional ability and rage issues. We learned from an early age that this was no way to behave on the court, or in any sporting event, for that matter. My family culture prized a good attitude over a superior score every time.

When my *fiancé* threw his racquet, I turned, gathered up my things and walked out. My mother had taught us this maneuver: *When things get out of hand, just leave the room.* She handed out techniques for non-confrontation the way some mothers dole out their favorite jewelry. Her best advice for a happy marriage?

Don't fight. But I didn't want to fight. I wanted a different man. Pure and simple. Seems like I took the ol' happily-ever-after option a bit too hastily, and it showed in the disclosures I hadn't noticed at first. *Caveat sponsa,* people. If I had had to sit for an exit interview, I would have said *our styles conflicted*, winking conspiratorially. Irreconcilable differences, it turns out. Balls jokes.

People I dated were always urging me to give them feedback about their overall 'performance,' but my feeling remains that feedback when you are dating someone just messes with the experiment (see Schrödinger's Cat), in which I discover who the Hell you are and whether we have legs. He had shown me who he was, and I was no longer interested. Like, forget the whole thing. He chased after me, followed me to my car.

"We've got a runner!" He yelled into the night. And that was the beginning of the end of the goalkeeper with the big mouth and the bad attitude. (You may be understandably asking yourself, *which one?* I wouldn't blame you.) But don't worry, he met someone a month after I called things off. Apparently, there was another mortal coil they had to consider on her side of the family, so they rushed to the altar after eight months. They lasted a year. He should swear off dating runners.

John D. Rockefeller Jr.'s Indoor Court

It was on a tennis court that I had one of the biggest epiphanies of my life. I was returning a difficult shot that had already sped by the ideal point of impact. I had to wing a forehand that was sheer improvisation, not the skilled return shot you see in televised tournaments and want so badly to emulate. I was defendant, judge, and jury as I reviewed my performance in the moments before the next shot. Part of me was annoyed with my passive approach, another part was critical of my poor technique, while the defense team pointed out the uneven contest between me and my higher-ranked opponent. The mental struggle ended when I took the next shot early and ferociously, which resulted in a winning passing shot and the subsequent moment of elation, then enlightenment. *From now on*, I decided then and there, *I am not going to let tennis happen to me. I am going to happen to tennis.* I started winding up my stroke sooner, hitting earlier and with more purpose, attempting more drop shots, and ultimately winning more points.

By bedtime, I had substituted 'life' for 'tennis,' and have been trying to "happen to life" ever since. Happening to life means not playing the victim of my circumstances. Instead, circumstances become the straw I spin into gold, to harken back to a fairy tale about someone spinning straw into gold. I don't remember the rest, but I think she is a princess locked up somewhere and she pricks her finger. Things work out for her, and they have worked out for me.

Please don't confuse happening to life with getting your way. Think of happening to life as an explosion of purpose. Which brings me to boarding school, and to the Rockefellers.

There are many reasons kids get sent to prep school. Some of the most common are 1) Their parents were sent 2) Their parents are separating 3) Their parents need four years of alone time 4) Their parents feel the need to do what other parents like them do 5) Their parents can't handle them. Far down on the list is to prepare for college because you can do that anywhere if you are motivated enough. If you asked my father, we went to boarding school because of Reason Number One but if you asked our mother, she liked to say she wanted to 'outsource discipline' through the critical teen years. Above all, both of our parents felt that sending us to excellent schools would allow us to meet interesting people.

In my case, the interesting people ran the gamut from a scholarship kid off a Native American reservation to a couple of Rockefellers who were first cousins. This story is about the latter, and about happening to life. A play of mine was being performed off-off-Broadway, and one of my fellow Choate alums attended a performance. During the intermission she asked me if I was going to our former classmate's party at the Rockefeller estate. It was intended to get the class excited about our upcoming Choate reunion later that spring, but I was just excited to go back to Kykuit, John D. Rockefeller Jr.'s estate on the Hudson River, having last been there forty years earlier for the other Rockefeller cousin's unforgettable graduation party.

Yes, I would attend, and yes, I would appreciate a ride. It was suggested I bring my tennis racquet. The follow-up question was, would I be needing a place to stay that night. Now, given that I had secured a ride there, I would logically be able to get a ride back again into the city, but that would be life happening to me and I wanted to happen to life so I acknowledged that yes, I would need a place to stay (and would take the train the next day). Only one other classmate "happened to life" that night and after a private tour of the outdoor modern art installations, followed by a joyous mini-reunion in the Tudor-style Playhouse, featuring indoor and outdoor pools and tennis courts, a bowling alley, a billiards room among many other attractions, my former classmate and I were shown to a three-story guest house, one of several beautiful dwellings dotted about the estate. In the morning, after enjoying a breakfast out of the stocked fridge, we happened upon our host delivering patio furniture back to the house where we were staying. We offered to help him with the rest of the cleanup. By the end of the morning, we had carted off trash, taken down balloons, and moved all the furniture back to where it belonged. It was time for some tennis. Nothing special— I just wanted to rally on the indoor court with its ornate mahogany fireplaces situated courtside that John D. Rockefeller Jr. had brought over from his short-lived eight-story mansion at 10 West 54th Street.

Fireplaces on the indoor court

I wanted to play where generations of Rockefellers had played before me. I wanted to hit a ball like a Rockefeller. I wanted to put away an overhead smash like one. It turns out, hitting a ball on John D. Rockefeller Jr.'s indoor tennis court takes the exact same muscles as hitting a ball on a municipal court. I'll just remember it more vividly. I have had the privilege of playing with a pal at his club in Brooklyn Heights (yes, that club), and that is the only other indoor court that reminds me a great deal of John D. Rockefeller Jr.'s indoor court, with its minimal floor space beyond the out-of-bounds. But pointing out that their court reminds you of the indoor court at the Rockefellers' estate simply can't be expressed in anything but the braying of a name-dropping arriviste. So I chose to write a memoir instead.

I didn't count on driving with John D. Rockefeller Jr.'s great-grandson from the estate to his family home nearby, where we talked about writing the entire way. He is a man of many talents and interests, and ever since that day gathering up the balloons in our school colors, and filling trash bags, we have become writing buddies. If I hadn't stayed overnight and helped clean up in the morning, I wouldn't have connected with this fascinating guy, whose great-grandfather founded the largest philanthropic foundation in our country's history, a man who surely knew how to happen to life and has passed it down.

Beginnings

My eyes blink open shortly before the alarm is set to go off, a skill I have developed to afford my husband that last half hour without interruption. After cursory ablutions, I use a flashlight to grab any last necessities and stumble out of the bedroom down the hall to my daughter's room, where she slumbers entirely under the covers. Waking her up and getting her out of bed is a multi-step process, involving cooing and soft lighting, increasingly urgent whispers, the promise of a warm car...and finally a slight edge to my voice. At her age, her sleep is vital to her mood regulation, but her early-morning lesson is in 26 minutes, eight and a half of which are taken up with the drive there. We don't want to leave her teacher wondering if we overslept (again).

I rummage for a pack of breakfast biscuits and fill a thermos with hot tea. The lesson is indoors, so I won't need to bundle up. I yank Yak Traks over my boots and clomp to the car, currently unresponsive under a coating of frost. I delight in hiking up the temperature to eighty degrees and blasting the fan; it is a tropical vacation for a few quiet moments.

She comes bumping out the door, dragging her tennis bag and hitching up her warm-ups, untied boots flapping, eyes fixed on the icy driveway. In the car, she munches ungratefully on a breakfast biscuit, scowling at the too-hot tea from my thermos. I don't ask her how she slept. It is irrelevant. She flips the radio on and turns it to something insistent and a little loud. I resist the temptation to turn down the volume, postponing our first altercation of the day. I let her take the lead on early-morning conversation, having learned the hard way that my initiative is neither welcome nor reciprocated. Like the family dog that suddenly turns on a visitor and then must be put down, she has surprised me more than once with her sudden, fierce responses.

But with her tennis coach, she is downright courtly, smiling demurely, going through his drills gamely, taking in his admonishments with a maturity and grace that I don't recognize. When her technique fails her, she half smiles and shrugs, then tries again. She is simply a joy to work with, according to the pro. A hard-working student with a steady disposition. After some 250 serves, many of which go into the net or out, she ends with a rally that resembles a game of fetch. She comes off the court glowing. Apps exchange money. She changes out of her sneakers and back into her snow boots and we brave the cold walk back to the car. She hasn't bothered to put her warm-ups back on. I don't comment on how cold she must be. Nearing the edge of town, she asks if we can stop for coffee. She has a Zoom meeting and won't have time to make a pot. She is taking the lead on a new client and wants to review the talking points for the meeting. (Tricked ya! You thought this was about a child, didn't you?)

In the middle of the pandemic summer, after a particularly grueling weekend of missing her breathless life in New York City, her friend group, young suitors who could have been hers if only flirting up close were still a thing, and taking it out on her family of origin, I was moved to speak my mind.

"You need a hobby. And I don't mean working out to Zoom classes. Or plowing through the classics. I want you to do something for the love of doing it, not because you feel you have to." Sometimes we parents get it right. Never mind that I put both kids in tennis camps when they were youngsters, that they watched me and their dad enjoy the sport their entire lives...that day, my 24-year-old daughter decided to take up a new sport, as if the idea were occurring to her for the very first time. Tennis.

That moment changed us. At least it changed our pandemic relationship. Four in a house that had briefly contained only two, with conflicting schedules and needs, plus errand protocols and shortages, telecommuting long hours, putting out fires seven days a week on the Internet, in the financial world, and as a first responder...there was truly nothing left over for interpersonal relations besides dropping in on a TV-viewing session.

When my daughter picked up my old Wilson Triad and asked me to hit with her at the local courts, it was like opening a new can of balls; that initial, promising pffffft that lets the compression escape, as the new balls spill out, a bouncing, fluorescent waterfall.

As a strong intermediate player, the very last thing on my tennis bucket list is a game with a total beginner. Yet standing in the summer sun tossing the ball at my daughter's awaiting racquet was a homecoming. I found patience like forgotten clothes that still fit. I dipped into reservoirs of goodwill, cheering her on when she connected, and showing her where she could get better results as gently as I taught her how to spell her name. Mastering the game of tennis quickly became something my daughter loves to do. She revels in the monotony of drills, all for the very occasional victory of meeting the ball in her sweet spot. And what a sweet spot! The grim isolation of mid-summer made way for the glee with which she improved almost daily. We did play nearly every day, though it was hardly "playing" for me. Her Apple watch was reporting close to 1,000 calories burned throughout my drills, while I stood in my spot, playing the same carnival game for over an hour.

But was it ever worth it to see this frustrated, thorny prisoner of the pandemic put down her old kit bag and pick up a tennis racquet. The frustration of sheltering in place fell away as her double-handed backhand took over. Now we go to the tennis club through deep snow and single digits. She uses her money she hasn't been spending on Manhattan take-out for tennis lessons. She practices her serve for half the lesson. Tossing, smashing, leaning, bending her right knee...but most days, we play together against the ball machine. She sets it up, being in charge of all things digital readout. And she provides the music if we get there early enough, and the second court is empty. The same insistent beats from the car keep us hustling on the court: three minutes on, sashaying back and forth, alternating cross courts with the alley; three minutes off, tossing, lifting hand weights, or shagging balls. We unplug the machine with plenty of time to clean up the court, grab our masks and exit the building before the next players show up, the Pandemic Way. Then it's back home for showers and client calls; both of us individually stronger, and together, enjoying a deeper shared connection than ever before.

Fireballs

When we moved 3,000 miles away to forge a new life for ourselves in a charming New England town, we joined a nearby athletic club complete with four indoor tennis courts. If it weren't for that club, I would not have survived the New England winters. There is nothing I enjoy more in the winter months than showing up in sub-zero temps and stripping down to a tennis skirt for an hour or more of heart-pumping tennis. It is the ultimate middle finger to snowdrifts and sub-zero temps. It says we are having so much fun and no ice!

I remember some of those early clinics I joined when we first got to town. There wasn't time to get to know the other clinicians (?) because it turns out I had a whole compliment of bad habits I needed to break. Forget friends—I needed game. After a year of drilling, I was finally ready to crack the code of the United States Tennis Association (USTA). I would see strong players out on the courts either in practice or facing off another team—you could tell by the fruit plates and sandwiches that were laid out in the common area that something big and important was happening on those courts. How on earth did these women end up on those teams? Who do I have to bribe around here to give me some information? Finally, an oddly reluctant tennis coach explained that those were USTA teams, and I wasn't good enough to play with them. (He might quibble with my recap, but that was the gist of our initial conversation.) Um, excuse me; I played on a USTA team back in Northern California. Granted, ten years had evaporated since that first foray into team tennis, but when I looked in the mirror, I still saw a USTA player. By the time I was playing on *three teams* a couple of years later (briefly, but still), I had convinced both of us that I was up to USTA team tennis. Hard work pays off, but we know this.

I would have liked to have known more about the team tennis earlier on. My husband has a management approach that borrows directly from the Golden Rule and applies to USTA politics. When you climb up the management ladder, you invariably encounter a 'bad boss.' As you move on, you get to decide whether to be that bad boss to someone else in a kind of cosmic revenge, or you can be the boss that you wish that boss had been. My husband has consistently chosen the latter. Shortly after I had finally joined my first USTA team, a new face appeared at a round-robin social at the club. So that she wouldn't be left standing all alone in a sea of people who already knew one another, as I once had, I introduced myself. She asked about teams, and I brought her over to meet my captain. Today, she (along with the captain I introduced to her that day) is one of the league's great captains. You can wait for the miracle, or you can help make it happen. For everyone's sake, *be the good boss.*

One early tennis friend told me about a team she joined, called the Fireballs, where they handed out and encouraged everyone to drink one of those nip bottles of spirits before their first match. I knew about hard liquor before a table tennis match, yet I wasn't sure I would be able to keep up with such a crowd. Peer pressure in your sixties is a thing, people. A year later, I was telling a teammate about the team that handed out Fireballs and she informed me that I was playing on that team. They had retired the name and the tradition by the time I had found my way to them. I should have known they were the Fireballs; practices were rowdy, the smack talk was rife, and most weeks, players met after practice on boats and in bars for some high-energy bonding. When one of my plays opened at a theatre in nearby Portsmouth, over a dozen former Fireballs signed up for dinner and a show to come support me. I joined them briefly in their private room at the restaurant, and they toasted me like a celebrity. They informed the waitress that I was famous. I was certainly known throughout that room. What a swell group of gals who really know how to form community.

Some of the Fireballs (aka Team Unmatchables)

Three years later, all my closest friends here are tennis pals (plus one private loan officer—you'll meet her soon). I even joined a virtual tennis ladder and have a monthly singles game with players from all around the region. One of them has organized a group of us to spend a week playing tennis in Cancun. I honestly can't think of a more fun vacation.

All of this because I kept up my tennis.

A Mental Game

"Love-love-have-fun!"

She doesn't turn before the toss. That means it's probably going to my back—oops make that a forehand squeeze drop swing step! Catch the racquet. Ow. OK backwards quickly quickly don't trip oh my gosh that time Mrs. What's-her-name...with the two kids I used to babysit...Mrs. Starts-with-a-T?—

"Fifteen-love."

She wore those bright white tennis dresses and the peds with colorful heel pom poms. First serve in, fine. Dammit. I swear that net feels high. Oh! Blooped right over! Thanks, net!

"Ha ha I didn't mean to do that!"

"Fifteen-all."

Mrs. Thompson. That's it. She was walking to the service line and never saw the ball, until she was balancing on it like a circus animal and then her tennis panties led the way to a very public dethroning. Dammit I need to FINISH the stroke. Thirty-fifteen already? Come on, now. It's comeback time just get it over the net nothing fancy ooooh I can get that if I push off NOW and then drop it cuz she isn't budging.

"Nice shot. Good hustle. Thirty all."

I need to do more drop shots. Aw for—

"Ad in."

She doesn't use her weight on that serve, which would work to her advantage. Just aim for her feet ok now don't look watch the ball don't look up...keep watching OK now you can look oh no—yes! Back to center! Now just lob it and breathe. If I make pork loin for Saturday, I can use some of the rosemary. We need to cull the herb garden. I have no idea what to do with half of that st—

"Oops, just wide! Nice rally though!"

She doesn't believe me. It was 100% out, no question. Why would I cheat. That would be disgraceful. Sometimes you think "did I call that right" but that's not even the case here. She needs the next point to prove she was right. Well, I need it too—

"Deuce."

I guess she needed it more. Everyone loves deuce. I hate deuce. I always lose them. If it gets to deuce, you'll cook my goose.

"Ad in!"

Come on, now, hard at her backhand. If she's the least bit thrown off—go! Nice. Like mailing a letter. Rush and intercept.

"Deuce!"

I'm getting another one of these skorts. Nice long leg, no chafe. Is that a dimple on my thigh? A thigh dimple? Is that even a thing!?

"Ad in!"

Ugh. All I need are three points in a row. No big deal. It has to be in a row starting now or she wins. Squeeze and up, now catch the racquet now get back to center. It could be the skort shorts making that dimple.

"Game."

Dammit.

Tennis is a mental game because you have so much time to *think* when you are rallying. I do some of my best thinking on the tennis court (which is why I am not a 4.0 player). And one thing I have often thought; if it weren't for tennis, I would have someone's bedroom window staring straight into my bathroom.

When we bought our house, it turned out that the line of trees directly above the back patio abutted land that had once belonged to the house but had been sold separately to a family who had plans for a monster house, which were about to be approved to be located on land that had literally never had a house on it. Wigwams maybe. A built structure, never. We only learned of the proposed building plans after we had signed our own purchase agreement, and were preparing to move in.

Just beyond the terraced garden out back was planned a looming edifice with a three-car garage, a basement, and all the trimmings. Unfortunately for the owner of this proposed new home, he was intending to build his architectural statement on the last lot in the historic district and there were some pesky regulations he was fudging in his design. The fenestration was off, the scale was wrong, and the mature trees they wanted to take out, that were protected unless otherwise waived through, numbered seventeen. (They marked each of them with neon orange paint and it was only a matter of a few votes in their favor to complete the massacre.)

Showing up somewhere with no friends, and worse, no school-age kids, who traditionally plow the way for new friendships among their classmates' parents...the terrible part about moving somewhere new with no kids to hide behind is the sense that you are a mere specter of your former self. That you may never again have the get-up-and-go to break into someone else's friend group. Why would anyone bother to invite you in? That you will spend the next decade on Zoom and Facebook-er-Meta with your old friends, making all your local conversation with the check-out folks and the guy who greets you at the dump. To this I say: get a grip.

I knew precisely one person in this, our new town: a tennis player I had met at our club in the next town over. Starting with that one acquaintance (now friend), I built a network of people who care a great deal about the wooded hillside to the south of our lovely old house, across the river from a beloved strolling park that feeds into the historic district. These people care a lot and let the Historic Commission know it. The permit was not granted. We ended up buying the lot. But only because my bosom buddy, the kind of dear friend you fear you won't meet when you move to a new town, a friend who appeared in my life out of the firmament, asked us one day if we wanted to borrow an enormous sum of money and the fact was, we desperately did. Banks won't lend to you if you don't intend to build on your land and we most certainly did not. We were what you might call desperate for a funding source when out of the blue, just as when she first appeared to me in a Facebook-er-Meta message, noting that we were both moving from the same town to the same town, as revealed to her husband by my husband on a public Facebook-er-Meta post. We met soon after I moved in, and she was my second recruit in the fight to secure the hillside and its mature trees. One day well into the battle, this earth angel texted me offering to lend us a sum of money—exactly how much we needed (which she didn't know), at a very reasonable 5%. They had money lying around after a failed real estate deal, money that was earning a fraction of the interest we could pay so it was a win-win, my favorite state of play. Now we have a traditional stone wall demarcating our property, as it had long been for centuries. The woods that used to supply timber to the ship-building operations on the river have been secured as an undisturbed home to deer, fox, beaver, mink, and even bear. They can stare into my bathroom all they want.

Then There Was Pickleball

An old friend was forced to relocate to a new town recently, in an unplanned later-life move. She had no obvious way to make friends, given her advanced age and empty nest. Short of organizing a campaign to block the permitting of an out-of-scale house in the neighborhood, there is only one way I know of to make new friends at our age. One word: pickleball.

Here's why. Unlike tennis, which takes the requisite 2,000 hours to get a solid game under your belt, with pickleball, you need only learn how to score, how to swing and how to stay out of the kitchen. *Huh?* You may be muttering. *The kitchen?* (Shout out to my college buddy who went to Pickleball Nationals in Indian Wells, CA this year in mixed <u>and</u> regular doubles. She has taught me everything I need to know to play like a winner. All I have to do at this point is apply it. Thanks, pal!)

I have heard the origin story of pickleball. A father of three was trying to keep his kids busy somewhere in the state of Washington with only a Wiffle ball, some ping pong paddles, and a driveway, plus a nearby pet dog named Pickle who no doubt wanted to join in on this fast, fun, smashy, slicey, social, not too aerobic teamish sport.

A recent statistic shows that where all other sports remain flat, pickleball adoption has grown a whopping 7% over a recently recorded year here in the U.S.

I can attest to the fact that I have been unable to find a can of tennis balls at any local retail outlets (pandemic-related supply-chain issues?) for months now but there are whole walls devoted to the sport of pickleball. It is catching up in terms of equipment up sales as well: these days, you can get a pickleball paddle for well over $100.

I went to see my friend in her new town and brought pickleball paddles with me. We had a tutorial down at the municipal courts (plus a parking dry run), then I taught her husbands (long story) after work one evening. They all know how to score, how to stay out of the kitchen (the seven feet closest to the thigh-high net) if the ball is in the air, and how to rush the net instinctively. Back in New Hampshire, my husband and I have been playing rollicking mixed doubles with friends who realized one day that their blacktop driveway measures the exact width of a pickleball court; we play loud and long surrounded by lawns and trees and herbaceous borders. That has led to me joining those vigorous seniors I pass at the local municipal courts on my way to my weekly singles tennis game. Now I, too, am enjoying a morning round robin, while the weather is still agreeable. True story: on my second visit to a Monday morning drop-in of some thirty pickleball players, I was invited to the holiday party. To quote Dear Old Dad one last time:

I ask you!

V.I.P. SECTION

In which anonymous contributors share stories involving paddles and racquets.

Paddle

If you are going to grow up in the cradle of historic New England, you might as well start out in Watertown, Massachusetts, established in 1630. A collection of stoic brick buildings line the center of town while white clapboard houses with screened porches and glossy black accents fuse along shady avenues a short stroll from the Charles River. Watertown was the picturesque backdrop of my early years. Hedges were trim, sidewalks were even, and blue skies were occasionally sprinkled with puffy white clouds. The landscape of my childhood pulsed and buzzed with life, occasionally foretelling rainstorms that spilled out from under a shimmering bright grey blanket. Even Watertown's municipal tennis courts were charmed; when my parents played there in my preschool years, they both seemed so carefree and in love. Perhaps there was more to the powerful rallies I witnessed from behind my toy trucks on the sideline, like bottled up resentment, or sexual frustration, but my young, beautiful parents seemed genuinely happy to be hitting the ball together. They always said the rain waited for them to finish, when I chased balls and raindrops around the court like their pet dog until it was time to head back to our two-bedroom cape on a half lot.

The family grew, along with my father's professional standing and we eventually relocated to Connecticut, to a bigger house, and where we joined an actual tennis club. By now tennis sent my parents in opposite directions. Dad played with the men, and Mom swished around in her tennis skirt with the ladies, whom my father liked to watch walk away from courts and cocktail tables. All the members looked and dressed alike, on and off the court. Whites were replaced by hot pinks paired with Kelly greens, plaids kept company with patchwork, a cheery palette served up on toned legs and browned forearms. The kids all resembled one another; neat little profiles sporting freckles and zinc stared down a future that refracted the comforts of a long-cultivated country-club lifestyle.

When winter came, and the courts were retired for the inclement months, you could still play platform tennis, or paddle tennis, on mini courts caged in chicken wire and elevated on heated platforms. Or, at least, the grown-ups could. I would see them breathing hard under the lights when I attended dancing school on Monday nights in the clubhouse. Then one Saturday, I was cutting through the parking lot on my bike when I came upon four girls my age playing paddle tennis. They had traded in their oh-so-short dresses and ruffled tennis panties for pastel sweaters with Norwegian patterns across their chests, two out of three little pearl buttons opened to form an arrow of soft wool and turtleneck cotton, pointing at future cleavage. Their turned up blue jeans brushed against the backs of their bright white canvas sneakers. Oh, to be sharing that cage with them! But I didn't own a paddle, nor had I a clear picture how the game was played. At my advanced age, I was unaccustomed to being a beginner at anything.

I was surprised and honored to be approached one morning by my father to join him as his paddle tennis partner down at the club. It was like being handed a cigar and asked to pull up a wingback chair.

Paddle tennis court in Rye, NH

I loved paddle from the first. I loved taking the ball off the walls. I loved the easy flow my dad and I developed on that half court, setting up shots and executing. Sharing any time at all alone with my father was a dream come true. At this point, he and my mother were not speaking half the time or yelling in whispers we could hear.

The paddle tennis stopped when my father moved out. I missed the game so much over the next two years that I finally decided to find myself another partner, a schoolmate. We clicked in different ways than I had with my father. We ended up entering tournaments. Part of me was chasing that great feeling of belonging with a partner on the court that I had felt with my quick-footed father. Part of me was reclaiming the game apart from the man who had disappointed my mother and abandoned me. The part that still hurt. I played with an ease and fluidity that masked an insatiable drive to win. To beat back my sense of loss? I started a team at the local high school. I arranged matches against our hated rivals in epic battles of archetypes on display.

Around the time I turned 17, my parents tried a brief reconciliation in the fall and winter of that year. My father and I became a paddle team again and entered a local tournament. We ran the table and captured the trophy. It was one of the happiest days of my life.

F.H.

Passion

Long have I loved the game of tennis. As an adult, I appreciate what it demands of players: concentration, strategy, cunning, physical prowess, lion-hearted competitiveness, self-determination, grit, and strength. When I was a child, tennis broke the tedium of long summer days and gave me something to strive for – shaking hands with the racquet (at first, a wooden Pancho Gonzalez; later, upon adolescence, a Wilson T2000, just like Chrissie Evert), learning to keep score, hitting a forehand cleanly.

I played with my parents and later, with my older siblings. Dad was terrible at line calls, really, a bold-faced liar now that I think about it. If you protested his suspect rulings, as I did hotly, he would twinkle and say, "You believe in the millimeter as a unit of measurement, don't you?' I would choke with rage. I wanted to beat him and beat him bad. He kept up his psy ops by declaring a serve "out," just as I was tossing it up. He was a master at needling and razzing on the court.

My mom had better manners, and I loved playing with her. She had beautiful legs; they were never more fetching than when she flounced in a tennis skirt. (Mom was not a flouncer by nature.) In her later life,

Alzheimer's muddled her. Once at Richmond's Hermitage Nursing Home, Mom insisted from her wheelchair that she needed to leave for her tennis match.

My first date with my husband was a tennis engagement. He told me he was taking me to his club, the Big Vanilla. There was a lascivious undertone to that. We played doubles on vacation together, prior to getting married, and he served a whopper – right into the back of my head. The ball hit me so hard, it flew over the fence. We still laugh when recalling how he rushed to my side, gasping, not able to keep from doubling over with hilarity, to ask, "Are you all right?"

We introduced our kids to tennis. I could see their frustration and competitiveness as they learned how to stroke the ball, and how to serve. They chafed at the time you spend picking up balls. It got me to thinking that maybe playing tennis as a girl really hadn't been that much fun. Now my adult kids remember our games with joy. Perhaps, like childbirth, youth tennis becomes gauzy, and you don't remember the pain of it.

I've travelled to the U.S. Open with friends from Roanoke for over a decade. Though I'm uncomfortable in hot weather, I find I can broil for hours in the heat, impervious to conditions, in awe of the players. Tennis is a sport of immense mental resilience, and instruction for life. Even though I no longer play, as I took up pickleball six years ago (it's easier to see the ball, and easier to cover the court), I have learned much from both pursuits:

Tournaments are never as much fun as weekend play. You're more relaxed, you haven't had to pay to play, and people don't show their asses like they do in tournaments.

Forget the last mistake.

Concentrate only on the moment.

People talk too much. I don't want to socialize. Let's play! This is serious stuff.

You have to be nice to everyone, even bad line callers (as I am now, carrying on my father's legacy).*

Inclusion is critical. Maybe a player is ancient, or has Alzheimer's like my mom did, as some of my weekly crew do. Treat them with kindness when they can't remember the score or make a bad line call (glass houses, after all).

It is magnificent to beat the boys. No more need be said.

Bend your knees.

Get a good grip, and you will execute better.

Never give up.

No one regrets being made to laugh.

* *One opponent showed up in a Trump 2020 hat. (I am a Democrat by profession.) My gorge rose, I felt seething hostility towards him, yet found, once the ball was in play, that he is a delightful player and person. You have to put that rot aside for the sake of the sport.*

G. M.

Prison

As a small child I would occasionally ask about my absent father and was always met with the same proclamation.

Your father is a criminal.

My mother was brutally vague with the details. The answer became completely reliant on my imagination, and so with a missing father and a tight-lipped mother, a masked bank robber seemed the most logical answer.

During this time in the 1980s, my family lived on a quiet tree-lined street in Palo Alto, California. A suburb on the San Francisco Peninsula, Palo Alto had ties to Stanford University and miles of bookcases. I only mention this because Stanford people always seemed to have an excess of books—and a bowl of citrus fruit on the table or counter.

Our neighborhood was Midtown and touted a department store where I bought marbles and a family-owned drug store where I bought candy. At seven years old these were my staples. Our family of six lived in an Eichler. Often described as "California Modern," it featured large glass windows, teak walls and an open floor plan. In Palo Alto, Eichlers were a lifestyle and my mother and stepfather fit the mold. We shopped at the co-op market, took camping trips in our orange Volkswagen bus and led a very hippie-influenced suburban life.

In third grade, our class was taught that every good writer asks who, what, when, where, why and sometimes how. With this knowledge I was emboldened to reopen the case of my missing father and began interrogations. *Where?* Prison. *Why?* He committed crimes. *What crimes?* The kind that make you a criminal. Further requests for information would inevitably be met with a gesture toward a living room bookshelf that housed the dictionary and a shiny set of Encyclopedias. If you couldn't get the answer from either set, by default, you were forced to move on. I relented and crossed my fingers that follow-up questions would be addressed in fourth grade.

I would periodically receive letters from prison. Each envelope was addressed to me in block print and always decorated with intricate pencil drawings with dark outlines and flowers or patterns with colored shading. In contrast the letters felt very formal, typed out and read like my father was just sending updates from summer camp; the food wasn't bad, he liked taking long walks, they were teaching woodworking and there was a cat that hung out in the prison office. One letter included a polaroid of the cat. It was a tabby.

By fourth grade my knowledge of crime expanded, not by way of essay technique, but thanks to the Ronald Reagan-era "Just Say No" drug campaign. During a mid-day spelling test a police officer casually walked into my classroom carrying a hard-shell briefcase. We tucked away our composition books and for the next 10 minutes he lectured about the many risks of drug use (prison!) followed by an officer-led chorus of nine-year old's making a pledge solemnly swearing not to do drugs. When the officer was convinced we were sincere, we were individually invited to come up, receive a certificate declaring our lifetime commitment to "Just Say No" and to examine the briefcase's contents. It was filled with clear labeled baggies containing every illegal drug known to man. Or at least now known to suburban fourth graders. I quickly tried to memorize as many names as I could and rushed to my seat to write them in my composition book: cokeaine, marijuana, LSD, crystal something-something, quaaaludes (how many a's?). I couldn't remember the rest. As my classmates were taking their turn at the suitcase my mind was spinning. Marijuana. My father had to be in prison for marijuana.

You see, at nine, I already knew about marijuana. This was just the first I had heard about it being illegal. I knew about marijuana because my stepfather grew it in our backyard and dried it in the outdoor shed. A large glass mayonnaise jar filled with marijuana lived on top of our refrigerator alongside a shoe box with crumpled aluminum foil that held a few pipes and a dish of loose change,

The masked bank robber scenario had really grown on me.

I quickly pushed my criminal father to the back of my mind and went on with daily life until a late afternoon in spring, while standing in the kitchen, feeling the sun shifting through the large windows at the back of our Eichler, pouring myself a bowl of cereal when my mother walked in to announce: *your father is getting out of prison and you will be seeing him this weekend at Mitchell Park.* Cue cartoon jaw drop, followed by a litany of questions and per the norm very few answers.

And so that sunny Sunday morning we rolled up to the park. My mother greeted a nondescript woman who was introduced as my case worker. She would be supervising our visits on behalf of the courts over the next months to determine visitation with my father. I have no recollection of this woman, so in my memory she presents as the teacher from the Peanuts cartoon. Wah wah woh wah wah. My mother promised to be back in two hours, and she drove away.

I stood on the curb with the lady and waited. A steady stream of people at the park made up a soccer match, kids on the playground and their minders, walkers, runners, sitters, dogs...a tall man with a beard walked toward us. He had crazy wind-blown brown curly hair to match the beard. He was smiling broadly.

My chaperone sat on a bench with a book while my father and I went for a walk. This person was a complete stranger. He asked questions and I answered. I felt like I should reciprocate but couldn't think of anything, my mind was blank. I asked about the tabby cat. He claimed I would like it. I agreed I likely would. He pushed me on the swings for a while, I climbed on large concrete turtles and jumped off the side. The lady came over and pointed at her watch. We walked back to the bench, had a hug, and with tears my father walked to his car. A few minutes later my mother pulled up and took me home. My father didn't really come up in discussion until the next weekend as we prepared for another visit.

Back at the bench, my father walked up carrying a tennis racquet and some loose tennis balls. He asked if I wanted to play some tennis. I had never played. Over the next hour he taught the basic rules of the game and I proceeded to do a lot of running around the tennis court. I held the tennis racquet in my right hand and practiced bouncing the ball on the ground with my left hand. Bounce ball, swing. Bounce ball, swing. My racquet connected with a ball maybe a dozen times, but this felt doable. By the time the lady walked to the fence pointing at her watch, my father, wild hair matted with sweat, was exhausted. He seemed happy.

Tennis filled our weekly supervised visits. By the end, my father was bringing two racquets and a can of balls. Bounce ball, swing with a stranger grew into a rally which grew into a match which grew into bonding over our games. As time passed our visits shifted beyond the court but I kept up my swing and continued to play through high school and on a team during my first year of college. When my sons were young, I would take them to Mitchell Park to learn bounce ball, swing but over time, each chose other directions. That was fine; in the end tennis was just about me and my dad.

T.H.

What's your story?

_____
_____
_____
_____
_____
_____
_____
_____
_____
_____
_____
_____
_____
_____
_____
_____
_____
_____
_____
_____
_____
_____
_____
_____

Printed in Great Britain
by Amazon

19613990R20104